Mutiny!

Why We Love Pirates
And How They Can Save Us

Also by Kester Brewin:

The Complex Christ

Other: Embracing Difference in a Fractured World

Kester Brewin teaches mathematics in South East London, publishes regularly in the national educational press and is a consultant for BBC education. His writing takes in fiction and poetry, as well as works that synthesise theology, philosophy and social commentary. He is currently working on a play based on his novel 'Nothing,' set in a London comprehensive school, and a new novel, re-imagining Steinbeck's *Cannery Row* in a deprived beach community in Essex.

@kesterbrewin | kesterbrewin.com

Mutiny!

Why We Love Pirates And How They Can Save Us

by

Kester Brewin

ISBN: 978-0-9559813-7-1

For Nic

Who first taught me to play pirate,
and took me 'on the account.'
Numquam Oblitus

[*I might be wrong*]

//

[*There may be errors*]

[*Child's Pirate Underpants, £3.49*]

1

Captain Roberts

'A Merry Life and a Short One'

Pistols Slung with Fine Silk

As Captain Roberts buttoned up his rich crimson waistcoat and breeches, carefully placed a red feather in his hat and hung a gold chain with diamond cross around his neck, he must have reflected on the extraordinary life he had had so far - a life that, now pursued by a hostile vessel, was very likely to end in spilt blood and terrible pain before the sun had set.

That morning, the 10th of February 1722, the Welsh-born mariner had breakfasted on board his ship the *Royal Fortune* on 'solomongundy' - a stew of meat, pickled herrings, hard boiled eggs, vegetables and liberal additions of wine, oil, vinegar and spices. His crew had come to him with warnings that they had sighted the British naval ship the *Swallow* rounding the cape, but, thinking they must be mistaken, he had taken little notice. The *Swallow* was a man-of-war, a 3-masted vessel of nearly 200 feet, with 50 cannon spread over a number of decks. It was one of the most powerful warships of its day. But he, and most of his officers, most of them already a little merry, thought the ship his crew had seen must have been their sister-ship, the *Ranger*, returning with more booty. Roberts soon knew he had made a mistake.

The *Royal Fortune* and the *Ranger* had amassed more than 4000 pounds in gold between them, which was not bad going, considering that Roberts had had to start from scratch not 2 years earlier. That incident had been another foolish mistake. He had set off from his former war base in a fast sloop with no stores, in greedy pursuit of a brigantine. Their pursuit was fruitless and the ship escaped, but Roberts was left with 40 starving men 30 leagues from his treasure and his main ship. With him not returning quickly, his remaining crew had thought him drowned or captured, and had reorganised themselves under a new leader, Captain Kennedy.

Roberts was not easily put down though. Recovering from his being blown off course in the sloop, attacking numerous ships and ports with his 40 men, he had built himself back up and was once again a fearsome and respected figure, much hated by the British, yet lauded by his crew and comrades for the 11-point 'Pirate Code' he had each of his men sign. Every member of the crew had a vote, no dice or cards were to be played, candles were to be extinguished at 8pm each night, pistols were to be kept clean, no quarrels on shore were to be carried on board, no man could break up their way of life until each had shared £1000 (around £20,000 in today's money) and if any man should lose a limb, he was to be paid £800 from the common purse.

That day in February he knew that his men would rather burn than see him caught and hanged, but, as he slung two pairs of pistols over his shoulders with a length of fine silk and took his sword his hand, he perhaps knew that the game was up. He barked his orders with boldness and spirit, trying to lift his men with a daring plan to close down the *Swallow*. They approached and received the man-of-war's fire. They hoisted their black flag, a skeleton holding a rod of flames, and returned fire, packing all of the sail that they could in order to run her by and then head round while she sank. But the wind shifted, *Royal Fortune* lost steerage and the *Swallow* came round a second time. Roberts was ready to fight, but gunners on the *Swallow* fired grape-shot at their decks and the sack of small lead balls scattered and hit him in the throat.

Knowing that death would certainly be upon him, he settled himself on the gun tackles and lay down to die. His helmsman saw a man lying down and went to berate him for laziness, but upon seeing Roberts, broke down in tears, crying out wishes that the next shot would take him. Here was his Captain, dead. The Captain who had told those who dared ask that:

> *'in honest service there is thin commons, low wages and hard labour; in this [pirate life], plenty and satiety, pleasure and ease, liberty and power.'*[1]

They had all come the same way: escaping the brutal slavery of the merchant navies for the democratic and free life of pirates, men who swore allegiance to no King nor Country, but only to fight for one another. '*Who would not balance creditor on this side,*' Roberts had said, '*when all the hazard that is run for it, at worst is only a sour look or two at choking?*' Grape-shot in the throat, or a rope around the neck - Roberts knew the risks he was taking, knew that most seamen who turned pirate lasted less than two years more. But he was undeterred. '*A merry life and a short one, shall be my motto,*' he said, perhaps choking up these words again as the blood spilled from his lacerated throat, hardly showing on the crimson waistcoat and breeches, but running red into the spray-washed deck, to the sound of booming cannon, falling masts and the approach of the British Navy.

Pirates Don't Change Nappies

Some two hundred and ninety years later, and many thousands of miles away, as I drive my son through South London to a party, dressed up not in the fine crimson and silk of a Captain, but in the striped t-shirt and sawn-off trousers of a proud crew-member nonetheless, I can't help but wonder - *what happened to pirates?* What happened to men like Roberts? How did these brutal and brave men, bloodied in battle, laughing in the face of the gallows, become suitable protagonists for a children's birthday party? When we arrive my son bounds into a hired hall with his tricorn hat and cardboard cutlass and is immediately set upon by a boy with a large black beard and buckled boots. This must be the fifth pirate party my son has been invited to in a year, which leaves it racing far ahead of the 'aggravated robbery' and 'ransomed hostage' themed birthday dos that are still to break their duck.

Was this what Roberts died for? Is the legacy of all his violent resistance a silly accent - Arrrrrr! - and a smiling skull and crossbones beaming up from a paper party plate? Is Jack the Ripper annoyed that his crimes have yet to be similarly softened into something approaching affection, and sterilised so completely that they are deemed suitable for infants and babies?

That the pirate 'brand' is everywhere must be significant, but what does it signify? We are living in tumultuous times, where uprisings against political and economic structures are spreading in number and growing louder in voice, and one cannot help think that Roberts should be leading a charge somewhere against 'thin commons, low wages and hard labour.' Is that him, a young black boy hijacking a container ship in the Gulf of Aden with an automatic rifle? Or is he actually in Brussels as leader of The Pirate

Party, enjoying the trappings of membership of the European parliament having won a huge section of the youth vote in Sweden?

The problem is that, as much as both of these could be him, so could the beaming cartoon caricature on the front of the children's book *Pirates Don't Change Nappies*. At least the Somali boys and the politicians are serious men fighting serious struggles. The romanticising of Bartholomew Roberts' life began even within his own time - ballads about 'Black Barty' were sung in his native Wales – yet surely he would be shocked at the way in which his rebellion and revolt against an oppressive and wealth-hungry Empire had been castrated into spineless, meaningless nursery pap.

Having died a gruesome death at the hands of a machine of war, the irony is that the real Captain Roberts slipped from view, while his caricature is now spotted everywhere. There are once again pirates sailing the oceans and pirates in politics, but the young pirates messing around at this birthday party may well be doing so to a soundtrack of dubious download origin, under a backdrop of a Hollywood film with a storyline buxomly full of swash-buckling thievery, burned to DVD using sophisticated encryption and digital water-marking techniques to prevent... piracy.

Perhaps my son's costume wasn't right. Perhaps the striped t-shirt and eye-patch was too obvious. Perhaps he should have turned up and circulated the tables with a plastic bag of pirated movies, or arrived in an inflatable rib, toting an AK47. The pirate moniker is confusing, because it is now suggestive of so many things, from computer hacking to media theft to hijacked shipping.

We Are All Pirates Now

Earlier in the day I had sat down to read with my son which, it turned out, was another act of rebellion. My crime? I read out passages from *Alice in Wonderland*. I did it knowingly, deliberately and pugnaciously, having checked a box to affirm that I had read the copyright notice which very clearly stated that, upon downloading, 'this book cannot be read aloud.' I was in full possession of these facts, but I chose to ignore them. With the news full of stories of banks committing robbery, and with big corporations demanding more work for more years for less reward, I decided to channel Roberts' spirit, and have a literary rebellion, because the law on reading aloud felt unjust.

Of course, we should never celebrate criminal behaviour, and it is not my intention here to paint a picture of pirates that is exclusively rosy. Pirates did some terrible things, and, no matter what their provocation and awful situation, their actions cannot be sanctified. But to deny any who break the law a place as important cultural signifiers rids us not only of pirates, but of almost all heroes we know. Why? Because one thing we can be sure of: if there is a 'forbidden forest,' then our hero is guaranteed to be bidden to enter it. Heroes break the law, because the power of literature tells us that the law *needs* breaking if it is to be remade more justly. Harry Potter broke 'official' Ministry of Magic wizarding law and was thus labelled a dangerous criminal. Only when he had defeated his nemesis did the scales fall from the eyes of the common people, and the terror of official Ministry law was replaced by the grace of the common spirit of magic. Or take Jesus Christ, who was, according to the law of the day, a revolutionary heretic who was quite rightly prosecuted by the religious authorities. The law had been broken, and law-breakers needed to face punishment if society was to hold together. But, quite explicitly, Jesus broke Jewish law in order to expose the fact that Jewish law was, in the hands of the Pharisees, broken.

When we ask where Captain Roberts' true descendants are now, we could say that they have taken up secret residence at the heart of our being - at the centre of that which we care most for. When I went ahead and read from *Alice in Wonderland* my guts were incensed by the choking copyright notice in the e-book and the spirit of Roberts in me deliberately and knowingly rebelled. It was a small act, but some lawyer in some office in some company far away decided that reading aloud was a step too far, and I, as a declaration of freedom, crossed the line they had drawn and disobeyed.

The problem is that the line keeps getting redrawn, and each time it is it draws closer to us. Once upon a time any printed or recorded matter was protected by copyright for a limited time. Now we have rights held in perpetuity, in all possible formats both current and yet-to-be-invented, with sometimes ridiculous restrictions on how we might use the material we have bought. All of us stumble over into petty acts of piracy because the rights holders we deal with often leave us little choice. In the gospels we read of Jesus asking 'which of you when your child asks for an egg would give them a scorpion?' And when a child wants to hear lines read from a book, which of you would refer them to the copyright notice and turn them down?

A splinter of Roberts' spirit is in each of us. We are all pirates now because, in these times of increasing corporate greed, cultural privatisation and financial oppression the fight that was once theirs has now become ours. Infamous in their time, pirates like Roberts were nonetheless distant characters, exotic figures from the far off high seas, firing cannon on Her Majesty's ships or mounting raids on trade vessels transporting goods around far-flung colonies. Their distant battles have now arrived on our doorsteps and flashed up on our screens. Pirates are now everywhere, taking up residence in radio stations, winning seats in elections, distributing films and music because their ancient battles against rich merchants have come home to us in our modern struggles navigating the channels of consumer capitalism.

Perhaps we allow our children to imitate these disreputable characters, and metaphorically take up our own cutlasses with smiles on our faces, because part of us knows that pirates offer something that speaks deeply to our human ache for justice. Roberts and his crew sing to us, in bawdy tones no doubt, of freedom, of rebellion, of high-spirited liberty from all in our culture that would seek to tie us down, hold us back and eke out of our pockets every last taxable dime that is owed.

Pirates like Bartholomew Roberts rose up because they had had enough of the violence and injustice they suffered at the hands of ship captains moving commodities around the New World, a 'triangle of trade' which funded the violence imperialism of Spain, Portugal and England. The aristocratic merchants and princes who controlled this proto-capitalism did so without thought for the slaves they abused nor the sailors they paid pittances to. Though skilled seamen were integral to the creation of fantastic wealth, they were completely disenfranchised from it, denied any rights to benefit from their labour.

As we will see, the emergence of piracy in the early 18th Century was intimately connected with this unfair monopoly which blocked access to the riches of the New World to any but the most privileged, and this takes us to the thrust of what is to follow here, for I want to argue that pirates emerge *whenever* economies become 'blocked.' To put it another way, wherever we see piracy we are looking at a system in trouble, a trading structure that is unjust, perhaps because it has taken something that should be the 'common property' of all people and locked it behind a pay-wall, perhaps because it refuses to share the spoils of wealth with those who have laboured so hard to create it.

And across the globe in the past two years we have seen an extraordinary explosion of 'pirate' activity. We see them emerging throughout the Arab world in the uprisings against oppressive regimes that have swept across Libya, Egypt and Tunisia. We see them in the protests against brutal working conditions beginning to become visible at the huge electronics factories in China. We see them in the student protests at the commercialisation of education in London and Paris. Throughout the world people are rising up to challenge the status quo, the scales falling from their eyes as the quiet agreement between workers and financiers collapses, and people realise that all is not well. The 'Occupy' movement of protests was born from this ancient cry of frustration when the '1%' end up gaining so much through the labour and sweat of the '99%' - and is amplified when the 1% so quickly turn to the little that the 99% have to prop up their regimes when the markets turn bad. These new pirates, living under canvas rather than sailing by it, were demanding no more than a little unblocking, an equitable sharing out of the wealth they had worked so hard to create.

It is not hard to imagine Roberts among their ranks, but I want to argue that his other sightings show us places where 'unblocking' needs to be done too. By looking at the history of broadcast and print media we will see that true pirates - not common thieves or extortionists - function not just as *economic bandits*, but also as *cultural heretics*. Their rebellion is not simply about fair trade, but unjust social structures. Where the young, the black, the gay and the voiceless find their path blocked, pirates will emerge and raise merry hell - whether in parliaments or theatres or radio stations, or even on the printed page.

Following Roberts from economic and media piracy into children's fascination with pirate life, into the fray we will then lead *Peter Pan* and *Luke Skywalker*, and explore how piratical works of unblocking go beyond economics and cultural regeneration, and into the depths of human maturity and personal development.

Finally, for nothing is sacred to them, we will see that pirates may well have raided our holy places too, and how it could be that a pirate-reading of *The Odyssey* and the parable of the Prodigal Son could lead us into a new understanding of faith in a world where religion is the 'blocked' institution to beat them all.

The blood still weeping into their fine clothes, the nooses tightening around their weather-beaten necks, the spirits of the dying pirate captains and crews lifted from their battle-scarred bodies and stole into banks, governments, radio stations, publishers, schools, and even to the innermost parts of our homes. We have welcomed them in because we instinctively know the work that they can do. As our economies lurch from crisis to crisis we know that they can help us resist the encroaching demands of the bankers and money-men. As our culture is narrowed and privatised, our folk histories copyrighted and our ancient music quantised, we know that they can help us clear a little ground and dance a while. And as we struggle to mature in an infantilising world of health and safety and legal liability, of fundamentalist preachers and narrow-minded teachers, we know that they could help us commit healthy mutiny, to grow up and cast off our immature and childish ways and become the integrated human beings that we each are.

But we have many seas to cross first, and before we reach those far shores we need first to return to the *Royal Fortune*, the legends and wild stories of Captain Roberts' 'golden age' of piracy and examine more closely who these pirates were, and which hell they had sailed from.

[*Pirate Baby Pacifier, £8.99*]

2

Captain Teach

A Brief History of Piracy

'The very negation of imperial social order'

18 months before Roberts was ambushed and killed, another notorious pirate was drinking into the night with his crew, again ignoring intelligence that said that two sloops were nearby and out to attack him. On the morning of the 22nd of November 1718, Captain Teach finally realised the danger that he was in, and prepared himself for action. As was his way, he dressed in his finest coat and twisted his long, dark beard into small tails tied with ribbons, some of which he then turned about his ears. He had a brace of pistols slung in bandoliers, and, as he took his place for battle, ignited fizzing matches that he stuck under his hat and into his beard, making his already dark face flicker and shadow with unforgettable menace.

A few months earlier there had been a rumour that Teach's ship was carrying an extra man, who had been spied above and below deck - a man not recognised by any of the crew. One wrote that 'they verily believed it was the devil,' and, as Teach stood now to face Lieutenant Robert Maynard and his British Navy sloop the *Ranger*, he might well have wished the devil to be among those who fought for him. For Captain Teach, or Blackbeard, as he was fearsomely known, had run aground in the Ocracoke Inlet and was unable to get away. Bravely, Maynard ditched his water and other supplies in order to lighten his vessel and was able to approach under oar. Blackbeard fired on him, broadside, and around 20 men were killed or wounded, yet still they approached and came alongside. As Maynard and the crew of the *Ranger* made to board, Blackbeard threw improvised grenades at them, which smoked and sprayed iron shot. Undeterred, they clambered aboard and engaged in a fierce hand-to-hand battle. Blackbeard had fourteen men with him, Maynard just twelve, and the fighting was so gruesome that 'the sea was tinctured with blood round the vessel.'[1] Blackbeard himself received no less than twenty-five wounds, five of them shots from pistols, and yet he fought on until, just as he was re-cocking one of his guns, he fell down dead, at which the rest of his crew either gave up life with him or jumped overboard and begged for mercy.

The crew who survived were taken alive and Maynard returned victorious, Blackbeard's severed head mounted on the bowsprit, still dripping blood into the waters as they approached Jamestown. The devil had not fought for Blackbeard that night, but many considered Captain Teach's death to be the extinction of the devil himself, so greatly was he feared.

Just six years later, in May 1724, in a small bookshop under the imposing shadow of London's St Paul's Cathedral, a plain, leather-bound volume went on sale among the fine Bibles and illuminated religious texts that were the standard fare of the day. Published at the height of the 'golden age' of piracy, what it lacked in decoration it made up for in its arresting title. Captain Charles Johnson's *A General History of the Robberies and Murders of the Most Notorious Pirates* told the story of Blackbeard and the other pirates and was an instant hit, devoured by the same crowds who flocked to the banks of the Thames to see the bodies of freshly executed mutineers dipped in tar and strung from gibbets as a warning to all against rebellion.

It remains a raucous read, with characters that a *Marvel* comic would be proud of: Roberts we have heard from, but he is joined on the page by Captain England, Captain Low, Captain Kidd and Anne Bonny all vying with one another in the details of their most gruesome acts. In one scene, Captain Skinner is reunited with a crew he'd abandoned:

> *'The men laid hold of the captain, made him fast to the windlass, and there pelted him with glass bottles, which cut him in a sad manner; after which they whipped him about the deck, till they were weary [...] and, at last, because he had been a good master, they said that he should have an easy death, and so shot him through the head.'*[2]

His prose is decorated, but his knowledge of the leading pirates of the day too comprehensive for his writing to be dismissed as entirely fictional. (For a long time the elusive Captain Johnson was thought to be a pseudonym of Daniel Defoe, but this is now doubted and his true identity remains something of a mystery.) In order not to anger the authorities of the day, Johnson is careful to dismiss pirates as thieves and 'the enemies of all mankind,' but one cannot read his account without being left with the impression that the pirates he described - and perhaps knew - led exciting lives, full of adventure, and were to be admired for their spirit.

This tension between outright criminality and spirited rebellion is a thread that appears to run through the heart of so much pirate literature. Even the children's 'Ladybird book about Pirates' gets caught between sympathy and disgust:

> *'In those days a man might legally be seized in the street by a 'press-gang' and compelled to serve for years as a sailor in a ship of the King's Navy, often without his wife or family knowing what had happened to him. Sailors were badly fed and brutally punished, and sometimes they mutinied, murdered their hated officers and became pirates in well-armed ships. Pirates [...] were mainly scoundrels and a menace to all honest folk.'*

This attitude stretches back as far as the very beginnings of seafaring itself. Ancient Greek texts - Homer's *Odyssey* and *Iliad* included - mention pirates in this twisted-hero light. Thucydides, writing in 471 BC, noted that many island inhabitants turned to piracy for their own gain, and to provide for the needy, 'an employment not bringing disgrace, but glory.'[3] It became an increasing problem around the Mediterranean with the rise of the Roman empire, even causing food shortages in Rome in AD100 as the frequency of attacks became so intense. The authorities responded by turning ferociously against pirates, who were a genuine menace to their imperial plans.

These Romans were the first to attempt to project sovereignty over the oceans, rather than simply travel across them. Up to that point the seas were seen as unowned and unownable by any person or state; they were a true 'no man's land.' The Roman attempt to extend their empire to include the seas was bold, and completely unrealistic. The seas had no roads through which traffic could be channelled, nor any vehicle equivalent to a chariot by which they could be navigated precisely, reliably and speedily. Ships were at the mercy of tides, currents and winds, and the vast expanses of water meant that it was impossible, even until relatively recently, to police them with any effectiveness. As one Dutch lawyer wrote in

1702, 'The sea can only be considered subject as far as the range of cannon extends,'[4] and this idea that once offshore and outside of the range of a nation's military might, a vessel was effectively outside of its laws too, was widely held. (Even in modern times the massive majority of the earth's oceans is designated 'International Waters' and thus outside the direct jurisdiction of any one nation.) Yet the Romans were determined to hold sway over the seas, just as they did over the land.

This desire to control the oceans symbolised the Roman attempt at the type of imperial project similar to that of the English and Spanish so many centuries later: a vast trading system that channelled enormous wealth back to the ruling capital. Rome went to war against pirates because pirates were threatening their claim to ownership, not just of the natural resources in the lands that they had dominated, but of the routes by which these resources could be moved, and thus transferred into riches. Pirates thus stood for the Romans not as simply a nuisance, committing petty theft on the seas, but as a threat to the values and principles that underpinned their empire. It was they who wrote into their laws that pirates were *hostis humanis generis* - the 'enemies of all mankind.'

'The pirate,' historian Marcus Rediker has written, 'was the very negation of imperial social order.'[5] Pirates were the antithesis of everything that Rome worked for: respect for authority, hard work, ordered trade and deference to a divinely appointed elite. From early history we see the designation 'pirate' going beyond robbery to suggest a wider menace that could undermine the values of empire.

It is against this backdrop that we can consider why pirate activity so suddenly exploded in the early part of the 18th century as it was exactly at this time that England, Spain, Portugal, France and Holland were all battling to expand their empires in the New World. The English had been at war with France in the War of the League of Augsburg until 1697, and then both of them were at war with Spain between 1702 and 1713. For a young man of the time, twenty of the sailor's first twenty-five years were passed in an Atlantic world at war.

These wars were not about expanding their borders, but about the ability to trade. Slaves were taken from the West African coast to be used in plantations in the West Indies. Sugar and other commodities were then shipped from there to home ports in Europe, and ships then set sail for the African coast again. England, Spain, Portugal, France and Holland were all fighting fiercely to gain control of this hugely lucrative 'triangle of trade,' and vessels from each country did their damndest to rob and disrupt the shipping of those of others. There was little distinction between the navies and the merchants of these different nations: naval vessels, apart from attacking ships of enemy countries, topped up their pay by trading, and private merchant vessels were given charters by kings to attack other ships too.

It was into this melee of battling boats and rampant thievery that pirates threw themselves. They were men who had sailed with merchant or naval vessels, often press-ganged into service against their will. It was a tough life, with pitiful pay (that was regularly not paid at all) and rotten rations that barely sustained their strength. Their superiors were brutal men, who used violence to enforce discipline, ate fine foods in luxurious cabins, and accrued huge riches through their raids and trading. Given the enormous stresses these poor men were under, in the confined spaces of a ship far away from family and loved ones, it is understandable that they regularly spoke of mutiny. These men knew the cost of doing so. To go 'on the account' - to turn pirate - would mean placing an immediate price upon their own heads. But, given the terrible mortality rates for merchant sailors anyway, this would eventually seem less of a threat, and a small group might band together, kill the Captain and his entourage, and take control of the ship. They then needed to make a living, and so, just as they had always done, just as every other ship was doing, they attacked and plundered.

Yet they ended up facing vociferous, international condemnation and brutal punishment for doing so. Why was this? If royal ships were involved in raids, and privateer boats were too, why were pirates so reviled for doing the exact same thing? The reason is quite clear: they were doing so without being under the authority of any king. Having mutinied against their officers, those who had turned pirate had also, by implication, turned against the monarchy and the whole structure of authority above them. It was, in royal eyes, quite acceptable to plunder other ships and steal their booty, as long as that was being done so for the furtherance of the empire, so long as riches were still being channelled back to the capital. Pirates were 'the very negation of imperial social order' precisely because to turn pirate they had raised two fingers at those who commanded them. It wasn't their thievery that was so heinous, so unutterably villainous, but their self-determination and refusal to be governed.

Caught in a Machine from which there was no Escape

It would not do for the poor to taste liberty. It would not do for them not to follow orders. Their acquiescent sweat and toil was essential to the creation of wealth and the growth of kingdoms. Any dissent had to be stamped out, violently.

As the 18th Century opened, the single most important factor in the expansion of the imperial project was movement beyond lands and into the domination of the sea. It was the development of faster, better ships which facilitated this, and funded it through international trade. Yet these ships were complex machines. Constructed entirely from wood, and powered mainly by the wind - with some facility for manoeuvring under oars - they required a large and somewhat skilful workforce to keep them going. If the sailing boat was the engine of international trade, then sailors were the cheap fuel that was thrown down, put under immense pressure and burned in order to keep that engine going. It is no surprise that they exploded into violence.

The notorious pirate William Fly was led to the gallows in Boston on 12th July 1726. As with all such public executions, his death was not simply punishment for the crimes he had committed - the murder of one Captain Green - but an opportunity to warn others of the price they would pay if they too were tempted to go 'on the account.' Fly was given an opportunity to speak - an opportunity that his captors expected he would use to ask for forgiveness and show remorse. Fly would have none of it. Having complained at the poor workmanship of the executioner and retied his own noose, he went to his death unrepentant, using his moment to speak to warn that '*all Masters of Vessels might take Warning by the Fate of Captain Green, and pay sailors their wages when due, and treat them better*.' He had earlier ranted to the priest sent to encourage him to repent that '*our captain and his mate used us barbarously. There is nothing said to our Commanders, let them never so much abuse us and use us like Dogs*.'[6]

Fly, like most others, had turned pirate because he had had enough of the barbarity of his employers on the Royal ships:

'Sailors suffered cramped, claustrophobic quarters, "food" that was often as rotten as it was meagre... they experienced as a matter of course devastating disease, disabling accidents, shipwreck and premature death. They faced discipline from their officers that was brutal at best and often murderous.'[7]

All this in return for impecunious wages which were often fiddled, and all with no protection from the law, whose role was simply to back up the establishment and ensure a cheap and ready supply of labour to keep the economy booming. Here were poor young men who were often forced into joining Royal ships, who then found themselves, in the words of surgeon of the time, 'caught in a machine from which there was no escape, bar desertion, incapacitation, or death.'[8] He went on to note that the *Weymouth*, sent out on a voyage across the Atlantic to the West Indies and back, left England with a crew of 240, and returned there with fully 280 dead in her log.

These kind of statistics remind us of the horrific numbers of slaves who died in transit on ships from the coasts of Africa to the West Indies, and there is an awful connection between the slavery of the men and women held in manacles below deck, and the brutal treatment of the crews on deck who were forced to transport them. Clearly the slaves had the worst of it - locked in irons and unable to move around during a long voyage that led only to hard labour for no pay - but they must too have see the horrible treatment that sailors suffered, with regular deaths and terrible beatings given arbitrarily to both.

One of the key reasons that pirates were hunted down so savagely was that they caused enormous disruption to the slave trade. Pirates often attacked slave ships and offered those held below the chance to go free, or join them on their pirate adventures – which many did.

The Pirate Code

It seems that pirates and slaves gained some mutual understanding through their shared experience of capture and ill-treatment. In fact, it was the very culture of institutionalised brutality and violence in the pursuit of wealth that was fire in which piracy was forged. As with the Romans, the powerful within the emerging empires of Britain, Spain and Holland saw pirates as a threat to imperial social order. Yet these men were not turning to piracy as a way of making themselves rich. Pirates rose up in mutiny in order to escape the barbaric conditions under which they had been forced to live. Mostly uneducated and with a very limited set of skills, they then turned to the only thing they knew, the only thing they had been trained in by the Royal Navies whose Royal Charters gave them official license to do it: theft at sea. Pirates continued the work they had always done - but now they were self-employed. It wasn't that the navies were trading legitimately and peacefully and the pirates came in to disturb it. The navies and merchants were raiding one another, employing privateers to do their dirty work too. Furthermore, the trade in which they were involved was grossly unfair, involving slave labour, virtual theft of resources from indigenous peoples, all to raise an enormous profit to which the labourers who had worked to get it - the sailors and slaves - had absolutely no access.

Liberty and equitable access to the riches they saw every day is what drew many to piracy, and what is very clear is that they achieved that: life aboard pirate ships was far superior to that on the Royal vessels. Pirate ships routinely worked on democratic principles, with elections of officers and booty shared equitably between all those on board. The Captain Roberts we met in the previous chapter even had his crew sign up to a code:

> *ARTICLE I - Every man shall have an equal vote in affairs of moment. He shall have an equal title to the fresh provisions or strong liquors at any time seized, and shall use them at pleasure unless a scarcity may make it necessary for the common good that a retrenchment may be voted.*
>
> *ARTICLE II - Every man shall be called fairly in turn by the list on board of prizes, because over and above their proper share, they are allowed a shift of clothes. But if they defraud the company to the value of even one dollar in plate, jewels or money, they shall be marooned. If any man rob another he shall have his nose and ears slit, and be put ashore where he shall be sure to encounter hardships.*
>
> *ARTICLE III - None shall game for money either with dice or cards.*
>
> *ARTICLE IV - The lights and candles should be put out at eight at night, and if any of the crew desire to drink after that hour they shall sit upon the open deck without lights.*

ARTICLE V - Each man shall keep his piece, cutlass and pistols at all times clean and ready for action.

ARTICLE VI - No boy or woman to be allowed amongst them. If any man shall be found seducing any of the latter sex and carrying her to sea in disguise he shall suffer death.

ARTICLE VII - He that shall desert the ship or his quarters in time of battle shall be punished by death or marooning.

ARTICLE VIII - None shall strike another on board the ship, but every man's quarrel shall be ended on shore by sword or pistol in this manner. At the word of command from the quartermaster, each man being previously placed back to back, shall turn and fire immediately. If any man do not, the quartermaster shall knock the piece out of his hand. If both miss their aim they shall take to their cutlasses, and he that draweth first blood shall be declared the victor.

ARTICLE IX - No man shall talk of breaking up their way of living till each has a share of 1,000. Every man who shall become a cripple or lose a limb in the service shall have 800 pieces of eight from the common stock and for lesser hurts proportionately.

ARTICLE X - The captain and the quartermaster shall each receive two shares of a prize, the master gunner and boatswain, one and one half shares, all other officers one and one quarter, and private gentlemen of fortune one share each.

ARTICLE XI - The musicians shall have rest on the Sabbath Day only by right. On all other days by favour only.[9]

To the modern reader this may appear a brutal regime, but to the sailor who had spent time on a merchant ship, this was extraordinarily equitable and liberating. Whereas they had previously taken no share of the goods they plundered, even the lowest rank on the ship was now entitled to a share half that of the most senior (income multiples that would leave CEOs in the West in a cold sweat) and, moreover, they could expect the distribution of the plunder to be fair and untarnished by fraud. This use of 'shares' to distribute resources needs to be understood in contrast to the elaborate hierarchies of the navy, and the wage system that they used. Rediker notes:

'[Pirates] abolished the wage relation central to the process of capitalist accumulation. So rather than work for wages using the tools and machine (the ship) owned by a capitalist merchant, pirates commanded the ship as their own property and shared equally in the risk of their common adventure.'[10]

With a full-scale banking crisis, and the press full of reports about anti-capitalist protest, it may be instructive to explain very briefly what Redicker means here. Rather than using a barter system, where the fleece for a sheep might be exchanged for milk from a neighbour's cow, money developed as a means of 'universal exchange: the fleece could be converted into money at an appropriate exchange value, and this money could then at a later date be used to buy milk - or whatever the holder wanted. Marx later called this a 'C-M-C' transaction, where a commodity was turned into money, which was then turned into another commodity. The tension that arises within capitalism is that the labourers who we might imagine shearing the sheep to get the fleece for the owner to sell at market do not receive a proper share of the profits. Instead, they are paid a wage which is unrelated to the profits that they create for the owner - the capitalist. The owner has people to work for him creating commodities, which he converts into *more* money than he is contracted to pay his workers.

The secondary layer within capitalism is that the person with capital sees that they can alter the phase of the 'C-M-C' rhythm by one step into 'M-C-M.' In other words, they invest money to create commodities - not because they need them or they have any particular interest in them, but simply so that they can take them to the market to make more money. And the only way they can do this is by paying fixed ways to workers, and denying them the share of the profits that their labour suggests they are entitled to. Capitalism creates a separation; by enclosing profits for the capitalist, the connection between the labour the workers offer and the rewards they receive is severed.

This is important, because in protesting against capitalism pirates were *not* attempting to usher in some sort of communism. Rather, they were simply trying to restore the idea that their labour ought to earn them a fair share of any profits that that labour created. The defence of capitalism is that the capitalist is risking their money, and so ought to be rewarded for putting venturing and investing. Without this money pumped in up front there would be less innovation and exploration. However, in the specific examples we are examining here, sailors were risking more than their money. Dragged against their will into merchant navies, they had no choice in the matter, and it is this alienation of the worker from the fair rewards of their labour, and the sense that they have no choice *but* to accept this system that created the mutinous atmosphere.

Those in the navies were disposable components in the capitalist machine. Their labour was rented for a pittance by the ship's owners. By adopting the pre-capitalist share system, pirates were not simply using a more egalitarian pay structure, but fundamentally shifting their relationship to the work that they did and the tools that they used. Pirates were anti-capitalist protestors, but their protest, they knew, would be met with terrible violence that puts modern 'kettling' tactics into some perspective. Moreover, they went beyond protest to model a new, fairer way of work and life, and lived it to the full.

This new mode of being had a further reach than just fair remuneration. Serious injury in Royal service would have meant abandonment in port (and thus no pay); now an injured sailor could expect to receive compensation on a scale that was unheard of. In modern terms, pirates could expect to receive around £20,000 for loss of a limb, or £3000 for a serious flesh wound. Having suffered routine beatings and brutal treatment, those who turned pirate could now live without fear of being struck while on board. With more equitable pay and some form of protection came improved conditions too: whereas the best food had been set apart for the officers, now access to fresh food - and good drink - was a right shared by all. It was expected that the Captain of a pirate ship would 'mess' (eat and socialise) with everyone else, and though the elected Captain might have the use of a cabin, all pirates could enter and choose to eat or sleep there. Decisions on board were taken by ship's council, which was the highest authority on the vessel. Having come from a situation where they were voiceless slaves, required to follow orders under pain of death, those who turned pirate were able to have a say in their own destiny through the election (and rejection) of officers and votes on every aspect of their lives.

Of course, this was still a horribly violent society - where disputes were settled with duels and punishments for contraventions of the code were severe. But this is all in stark contrast to life on the Royal ships, where there was no code - violence was meted out arbitrarily, there were no common rights to food and payment, and, despite having potentially been press-ganged into serving, there was no promise of compensation if that service ended in disability. Indeed, behind the comic caricature, some of the most enduring images of pirates that we have portray men with severe disabilities who are still given respect and responsibility on board ships, despite eye patches, wooden legs and hooks for hands.

Furthermore, one of the most well-known pirate stories - the blockade of Charleston harbour by Blackbeard - actually tells us something about the culture of care that existed on board pirate ships. We have already seen that Blackbeard was a fearsome pirate and manipulated his image to instil terror into his adversaries. As Captain Charles Johnson puts it:

> *'Captain Teach assumed the cognomen of Blackbeard from that large quantity of hair which, like a frightful meteor, covered his whole face and frightened America more than any comet that has appeared there a long time... such a figure that imagination cannot form an idea of a fury from hell to look more frightful.'*[11]

Johnson's language is colourful, but the impression is clear: Teach was a formidable sight. Despite this, and his and the violent reputation he clearly cultivated, he actually took good care of his crew. In May 1718, finding Charleston harbour unguarded he blockaded the entrance with his ships, and took a number of prisoners. One of them, Mr Marks, was sent ashore with some of Teach's crew with a simple demand: the town's governors should supply Teach with a chest of medicinal supplies within three days, or he would kill the hostages. No ships were able to enter or leave the harbour while this siege went on, and fear gripped the whole town while negotiations continued. Matters were not helped by the unfortunate Mr Marks, whose little boat capsized on the way into the harbour, thus delaying any return with the supplies. Teach granted him an extra two days to complete the task, but still Marks did not reappear. Only after a further day or so did Marks' boat reappear with the medicines and the prisoners were let go - the further delay had been down to Teach's crew getting so drunk that they couldn't easily be mustered for the return journey.

This pirate blockade has been become infamous, but the heart of the story is this: Blackbeard wanted medicines for his men. This in itself set him apart from the naval ships, who cared little about the health of the sailor-slaves who ran their men-of-war. They were expendable nobodies who could be replaced in any port, with a little violent coercion. What would be the point of wasting money on medicines, when fresh men could be mustered for free?

Blackbeard escaped with his medical supplies, but in doing so fanned the flames of anger against him even further. Those in power wanted him dead more than ever, and within a year they had their wish. Lieutenant Maynard successfully hunted him down and defeated him, but his victory was in many ways hollow: many of Maynard's own crew proceeded to turn pirate as soon as they had recovered from the toils of the expedition.

Libertatia

Why would these men have moved so quickly from a famous victory over a notorious pirate to turning pirate themselves as soon as they were able? Clearly the Lieutenant failed to impress his crew with his own values, and, having risked their lives defeating a mob of pirates, many of them took up with their 'enemies' and went 'on the account' with them because the pirate life they chose compared so favourably to the lawful life they had experienced under Maynard.

Sailors saw the enormous profits being made by merchants and princes, and knew that it was their slave labour that was sustaining this New World economy and the emergence of global capitalism. By turning pirate they were rejecting this system that had led to their oppression, and creating a life for themselves that stood in stark contrast. Yet pirates knew well the cost of their rebellion. They knew that rejection of the low status proffered them by princes and merchants, and refusing to be beaten down into no more than disposable labour units on board floating capitalist machines, would mean becoming a target for state violence. Pirates were hated vitriolically because they stood as powerful symbols of the rejection of the status quo. Rather than serve in silence and with reverence for their masters - whom surely God had made greater than they - they dared call themselves free equals, and stood up to act as such. For this arrogant rejection of the divine order of things, it was commonly held, they must suffer death.

Pirates knew that their life expectancy was short. Their declaration of freedom would burn brightly, but not burn for long. So they determined to make the most of their time in their 'short, but merry lives.' Their lives aboard naval vessels would not be greatly extended anyway, so better to have some fun while they could. Under constant threat of capture - and thus the gallows - pirates had to live under the radar as much as possible.

In our hyper-connected world, infested with CCTV, 24 hour news coverage, digital traces and paper trails, it is difficult for us to appreciate a world where information moved extremely slowly. While limited use of beacons permitted warnings to travel quickly over long distances, detailed information could only travel at the physical speed of the vehicle that carried it: running, on horseback, under sail. With modern day military reconnaissance, a drone can transmit live video footage of a location from hundreds of metres above ground, and operators can call in missile strikes to a specific area in a matter of minutes.

This is a very different world to that of the early 18th Century. News of a pirate hideout could take days or weeks to be relayed to a naval base, which then had to muster ships and crews and sail at the mercy of the wind and tide in bulky and highly visible vessels back to the place where pirates had been spotted. Pirates were expert seamen and often used faster, smaller ships than those typically launched in pursuit by the navy; as one frustrated Admiral put it, it was like 'sending a cow after a hare.' The British Empire had maps of the lands they controlled back in London (all Mercator projections that exaggerated the size of northern nations like Britain, while shrinking equatorial ones like the Caribbean and those of central Africa) but these maps suffered an even greater information lag, for at any one time scores of bays and inlets were quite definitely *not* under the authority of the crown. It was not until 1899 that the entire globe was properly charted - no more *terra incognita* - and thus prior to then there remained places which were literally 'off the map.' Pirates exploited this gap between cartography and on-the-ground reality and were able to set up communes along the coastlines where they enjoyed time ashore, repaired their ships, recruited men from plantations or logging stations who might be equally fed up with their oppression by wealthy owners.

The American anarchist writer Hakim Bey has called these spaces 'Temporary Autonomous Zones,' or TAZs. They were places which were liberated - for a time - from the distant authorities who technically claimed to be able to levy taxes and uphold laws. Bey explores these 'uncharted places' as spaces where there is 'an intensification of everyday life... life's penetration by the

Marvellous.'[12] The importance of their temporary nature we shall explore later, but suffice to say now that these pirate utopias were only able to exist because of the information lags that existed. The windows that these lags presented meant pirates could, for a while, exploit the ignorance of the Empire and live out their 'short but merry life' to the full.

One of the most infamous of these TAZ's was 'Libertatia.' It is unclear whether or not it was a real place, but its existence even in myth - perhaps fabricated by Captain Charles Johnson - at least suggests that such a place was credible, and fitted in with the portrait of pirate life that he was painting. Declaring itself free from control by any state, Libertatia is thought to have sprung up along the coast of Madagascar and functioned as a pirate colony with elected officials and a commitment to common ownership. The legend goes that one Captain Mission became disgusted with the decadence of the Catholic Church, and especially the Vatican itself, and turned away from this highly imperialist faith. He was joined on long voyages by a radical Italian priest called Caraccioli, who preached a social-gospel of universal human equality:

> *He shew'd, that every Man was born free, and had as much Right to what would support him, as to the Air he respired... that the vast Difference betwixt Man and Man, the one wallowing in Luxury, and the other in the most pinching Necessity, was owing only to Avarice and Ambition on the one Hand, and a pusillanimous Subjection on the other.*

Together, the story goes, they turned the whole crew of the *Victoire* pirate, and appointed Mission as Captain, declaring that they would share all things in common. They raided a Dutch slave ship, setting the slaves free and bringing them aboard as equals, Mission declaring:

> *'the Trading for those of our Species cou'd never be agreeable to the Eyes of divine Justice and that no Man has the Power of the Liberty of another; and while those who profess a more enlightened Knowledge of the Deity, sold men like Beasts; they prov'd that their Religion was no more than a Grimace!'*[13]

Sailing round the coast of Madagascar, they happened upon a bay with good soil and fresh water, and there created Libertatia - rejecting their given nationalities of English, Dutch, French or 'African' - and any denomination as slave or free, as well as religious labels too. Instead they called themselves simply Liberi - 'free ones.' It is reported that they developed a new language, mixing French, English, Dutch, Portuguese, native Madagascan and different African tongues too. Other pirates like Captain Tew then came to join them, and they captured more slave ships, setting more slaves free - even reuniting family members, and 'striking off their fetters with great joy.'

In the end it is perhaps irrelevant whether Libertatia actually existed or not. That it existed in the imagination of those who read Captain Johnson's book tells us that what Libertatia stood for stood already in the minds of those who rushed to read his tales of pirates and piracy.

Here was a place - real or imagined - where the working man's shackles of poverty and oppression had been cut off.

Here was a place where people of different races and languages were united in one thing: their struggle against forces that had enslaved them in the service of an Empire that wanted only to use them like disposable cogs in a machine.

Here was a place where the benefits of their labour could be shared by all, rather than stolen from them in beatings.

Here was also a place where sexual orientation could be freely expressed. As the historian B. R. Burg has shown in *Sodomy and the Pirate Tradition*, homosexuality was freely chosen by some groups of sailors. That it was condemned by the Royal Navy was not out of an ethical or moral objection, but because sexual activity of *any* kind distracted the mariner's from his labour.

Here, then, in Libertatia, for almost all of Johnson's readers would surely have heard something of the Bible too, was a glimpse of heaven, of the 'new Jerusalem' where there was 'neither Jew nor Greek, male nor female, slave nor free.' This heaven existed - but existed far across the sea. In the age of the jet plane and ocean liner it is difficult for us to appreciate the mystique that the vast seas held for people of this time. Here were watery spaces so huge that they were beyond comprehension. To launch onto the ocean meant opening oneself up to enormous danger, diving into a mysterious place from which invaders and strange spices came. Crossing the sea meant disappearing from life and community for weeks or months at a time. It was, in a very real way, like dying, and the prospect of leaving London, with all its rules and hierarchies, and landing on the shores of Libertatia would drip heavily with Christian imagery of moving from fallen earth to heaven.

Yet the effects of heavenly Libertatia were felt in earthly England. Seeping back through the pages of Johnson's book and into the hands and minds of Londoners were these stories of bands of free men outwitting the navy and defying the authorities far away on the oceans. Through his hugely successful history and the stories told in streets and taverns, the battle that pirates fought against the princes and merchants was brought back from the distant seas, onto land, and into urban myth. These were people who knew all too well about oppression and over-bearing superiors, for England had been the scene of long-running skirmishes between rich traders and labourers, who were unfairly excluded from a share of the takings.

Piracy, in other words, already had a long history on-shore as well as off. The free-spirited mariners who cast off the yokes of their captains had their equals in and among the poor of the streets of London, who were beginning to rise up against their oppressors too.

For the Benefit of the Poor

In 1707, just before the years of huge increase in Atlantic piracy, a London printer who became known as 'Henry Hill the Pirate' began selling poems, sermons and leaflets for as little as a halfpenny - a fraction of the usual sixpence that 'official' publishers charged. His motivations were clear from the motto he printed on each pamphlet: '*For the benefit of the poor*' and his business model - keeping material costs and per-copy profits to the absolute minimum - suggests that he was not just out for personal gain.

Like the sailors on the merchant ships, Hill was also working in an industry that was ring-fenced for the benefit of the few. At the end of the 17th century the Licensing Act in England served as a comfortable deal between the governing monarchy and the guild of printers known as the Stationers' Company. The act limited the number of 'master printers' in England to no more than twenty, restricted the number of presses each publisher could run and the number of apprentices they could employ. No printing was allowed to be done except in London, York, Oxford or Cambridge, and these select printing houses were granted monopolies on printing the high-selling books of the day - the Bible, legal works, almanacs and basic school books. In return for this privilege - which earned them huge sums of money - the master printers censored any other material they printed and made sure that nothing that they published nothing that criticised or questioned the Crown or the government - or the Anglican church that was so deeply embedded in both.

And yet there was sharp criticism of the ruling classes, and the ecclesiastic authorities too, and this is where the pirate publishers came in. Henry Hill and the many other unofficial printing houses were not going to tow the line with the authorities, nor with the Guild of Master Printers who kept all of the profitable work for themselves. They printed cheap editions which disseminated information among those who could neither afford the expensive official news-sheets, nor wanted to read heavily censored and biased pieces which said nothing about the reality they experienced far from the centre of power and influence.

So when Hill and others put out these very cheap pamphlets it stood as an act of piracy because it resisted the 'imperial social order' in two fundamental ways. Firstly, by printing censored texts they were protesting against the Crown's right to decide what people should be allowed to read. Secondly, by printing very cheap copies of protected works they were protesting the guild printers' monopoly over popular editions. Just as on the high seas, state reaction was violent: houses were searched, printing presses smashed and huge volumes of illegal books were confiscated. Yet printers who were excluded from the tiny circle of privileged guild members had little choice but to continue in their piracy. The monopolies kept them in poverty, and without being able to print versions of popular works they would have been unable to trade at all. In parallel with William Fly, they were vocal in their demands for more equitable treatment, but their demands long fell on deaf ears.

However, the law did eventually begin to change. The Licensing Act was allowed to slip in 1695, but it was only in 1710 that the Statute of Anne was passed, which relaxed some of the monopolies that guild printers had enjoyed, though not on works that had already been published. More radically this new law created, for the first time, a limited period of copyright - which was set at 21 years. For complex legal reasons it was disputed whether this limited period applied in Scotland, and thus after 1730 - as soon as the 21 year period had lapsed - Scottish printers began to produce huge numbers of popular works at knock-down prices and send them over the border to northern English towns. This created a long-running legal dispute, which was only resolved in 1774 with the case of Donaldson vs. Beckett. This landmark case effectively marked the end of perpetual copyright in English law, but in doing so created the idea of the 'public domain' - the ever-expanding body of work that is outside any copyright control and can be distributed and printed by anyone at any price (leading to me, in 2011, being able to buy an e-edition of the complete works of William Shakespeare for just 79p)

This rather arcane legal battle over copyright and censorship is important because of the ripples it sent out across the Atlantic to emerging nation of the United States. In 1886, in an attempt to curb piracy of works across international borders, Germany, Belgium, Spain, France, the United Kingdom, Italy, Switzerland, and Tunisia signed the Berne Convention for the Protection of Literary and Artistic Works. The US was notably absent from the signatories. They had, in 1790, created a copyright law based on the Statute of Anne (though reducing the copyright term to 14 years) but this *only* granted copyrights to US citizens. As Bodó Balázs has written in a history of book piracy:

> *As a major importer of British titles, this clause created a massive subsidy for US publishers and helped establish a de facto cultural policy of cheap books, which in turn became an essential component of mass public education.*[14]

We shall explore this in greater depth in Chapter 4, but here we see laid bare a founding principle of a nascent American nation: contravention of copyright law for the benefit of the common people. It wasn't that they disagreed with copyright *per se*, just that, under the particular influence of Benjamin Franklin, the founding fathers knew that access to cheap books and the free flow of information was going to be central to the creation of a well-informed liberal democracy.

It was another 100 years before the US finally signed the Berne Convention - a century in which the country was condemned internationally for their piracy. (Amusingly, the Netherlands refused to condemn publishers who translated Dutch copies of *Gone With the Wind* in 1947 because of the US's refusal to grant similar copyright protection to Dutch works) It was a claim that was strongly rebuffed on the grounds of freedom of information and the promotion of education. As one commentator put it in 1886:

> *All the riches of English literature are ours. English authorship comes to us as free as the vital air, untaxed, unhindered, even by the necessity of translation; and the question is, Shall we tax it, and thus impose a barrier to the circulation of intellectual and moral light? Shall we put up a dam, to obstruct the flow of the rivers of knowledge?*[15]

The Pirates of Puntland

From the reports of Thucydides, through the lives of Captain Roberts, Blackbeard and Henry Hill there is a common thread: whether in printing or the merchant navies, pirates emerge to rise up against inequitable monopolies and the violent systems of oppression and do so to free the flow of goods and information 'for the benefit of the poor.' Though this holds true for the piracy of the early 18th century, we need to explore whether this principle can be extrapolated to explain modern pirate activity too.

What is clear is that, after many years in the shadows, ocean-going piracy is once again right in the headlines. The Gulf of Aden, off the coast of Somalia, has seen hundreds of vessels - from privately owned yachts to enormous oil tankers - boarded and held hostage by pirates. The international response has been typically forceful, with task-forces being set up to patrol and protect vessels (a job they admit is virtually impossible in such a large area - sending a cow after a hare again) and rescue missions being attempted by heavily armed elite forces.

The question that appears to have been missed is why pirates have emerged in Somalia - and the region of Puntland - at all. Rather than asking what may have caused these young men to risk their lives in this way and how we might look to stop them wanting to turn pirate, those in power have mostly focused on the evils of piracy and the violent ends these people will meet if they persist, echoing their ancestors from 300 years ago.

The story is by no means simplistic, but, while there are certainly few angelic 'Robin Hoods' in the region (as Cutter Hodierne has shown in his Sundance-winning short film 'Fishing Without Nets') there are voices trying to make a case for a more balanced view than the media have generally taken. While at a drinks party in Kenya a couple of years ago I fell into conversation with a senior figure from the UK's Department for International Development, working from the safety of Nairobi to help bring aid and expertise to the anarchy to Somalia. 'They are desperately poor,' he said between sips of gin and tonic, 'and the fishing industry that had sustained the coastal population has collapsed completely as a result of over-fishing by European trawlers and contamination by toxic waste.' This waste was dumped by other states and multinational companies who knew that, with the collapse of the central government and the subsequent virtual dissolution of the Somali navy, there was a political and coastal policing vacuum in Somalia that meant they wouldn't be caught. The fishermen of Puntland began to band together and try to defend their waters themselves, but with the stocks exhausted by greedy fishing boats they soon gave up hope. Our Man (not) in Somalia was phlegmatic: here were redundant, impoverished fishermen sitting on the beaches of their neutered sea, watching huge ships cruising past carrying oil and fine things to the very people who had savaged their only means of economic engagement.

What choice did they have? Life in Puntland is hard enough. The container ships loaded with electronic goods and cheap toys may be just a few miles off their shores, but they might as well be light years away: they come from a world which is utterly blocked to these young Somalis. So although we must not *sympathise* what they have done, we must try to *empathise* with at least the first wave of these modern day pirates.[16] Piracy for them was perhaps not so much about greed but reparation – a shore tax to pay for the damage that had been done. Having seen the capitalist world exploit them, pillage the only resources they had and leave them for dead, piracy was a desperate act, a way of highlighting their fight for survival to the international community and moving them a little way up the list of priorities. Their hijacking of vessels is a violent extension of the M-C-M rhythm that the capitalist system runs on: they take hold of a commodity by force, and demand money in exchange for it.

The violent response of the international community's attempt to defend and rescue ships is in contrast to the actions of the pirates themselves who, until recently, used the threat of violence but appeared very reticent to carry it out. By way of example, in 2008 an article in *Vanity Fair* outlined the capture of the French luxury yacht *Le Ponant*. On the surface the story had everything that the pirate media storm would want: an exclusive sailing boat, carrying only 60 or so passengers at any one time, with a lithe, highly cultured French crew of both sexes. While these sailors took the boat from the Indian ocean to the Mediterranean, the empty vessel provided a perfect place for maritime trysts to flourish, and with a top chef on board and a cache of excellent wine, it was portrayed at the time as an idyllic journey that the pirates brutally interrupted. But, as the piece by journalist William Langewiesche explored, the truth of the crew's life was a little more complex, if shockingly familiar:

> *The wages were low, the hours were long, and no retirement benefits were provided. During rotations ashore there were no wages at all. These terms were non-negotiable. They stemmed from the culture of a global shipping industry which over the past 60 years has pursued profit and efficiency in part by ridding itself of labor unions, and more fundamentally by freeing itself from the constraints of the nation-state and its laws.*[17]

It turns out that *Le Ponant* was registered in the loosely held French protectorate of Wallis and Futuna, a tax haven that meant that the boat could fly the French flag – with all the romance that held for wealthy charterers – without having to abide by any French labour laws. It was into this situation that a group of Somali pirates came, boarding the boat and demanding $2.5m. The female members of the crew had been instructed to hide in the bows of the ship, but after a day or so they voted to come out. Ahmed, the pirates' leader was hugely offended:

> *"We do not touch women! We want money!" Referring to himself and his men, he said, "Robbers! Not terrorists!" Ahmed escorted the group aft to the luxurious lower lounge, where he ordered that the women be provided with water and food. When the water arrived, he sent it back for being lukewarm.*

Pirates, it seems, still have their code - and those in power have theirs. French forces tracked *Le Ponant*, and 8 days all hostages were released without incident. The pirates were tracked by French helicopters, and chased onshore into the desert, where a sniper disabled their get-away vehicle. A fight ensued, which some locals said claimed the lives of three people, but this was denied by the French. Six pirates were captured and flown to Paris, where they were tried and imprisoned.

Many Somali pirates have been killed in the battles that have gone on over ships like *Le Ponant*, but until much more recently, when organised gangs with international connections have begun to dominate activity in the region, no hostages had been killed, the only casualty being a French yachtsman who was shot by his own forces as they boarded the boat in a botched rescue attempt. It is perhaps unlikely, but one cannot help wonder if the pirates' reticence to use violence was because they were aware that, like them, those working the vessels were pawns in the game of global capitalism who were, unlike the goods they shipped, dispensable to the corporations who employed them. Either way, I believe we can see the pirate line running clearly from the brutalised 18th Century sailors to the impoverished fishermen on the shores of the Gulf of Aden: capitalism had screwed them, and they were not going down without a fight.

Radio Is My Bomb

Modern day Somali pirates have taken the mantle of their 18th Century wave-riding forebears like William Fly and Captain Roberts. Who has followed in the footsteps of the book pirate, Henry Hill? Hill's piracy takes us away from the ocean and into the wave of illicit publishing that swelled against the state-sponsored monopoly enjoyed by the Stationer's Company. The technology of printing, we must remember, was freely developed by Gutenberg and the state's arbitrary restrictions on its use has to be seen as oppressive, especially given that by 1500 some 20 million volumes had already been printed. Jump forward 400 years and we see that it may be radio that is the natural heir to Hill's piratic activity. Again, this was a technology developed by expert craftsmen, yet extensively explored by laymen. It was only around the outbreak of World War 1 that the United States decided to clamp down on these amateur broadcasts, as it wanted to restrict various parts of the radio spectrum for military use. (Indeed, during WW1 the navy deemed it illegal to own a wireless receiving set in the US.)

In the 1920's a group of six radio broadcasters and equipment manufacturers formed the British Broadcasting Company, which had an effective monopoly on the sale of wireless sets and the broadcasts they could receive. In 1927 this company was wound up, and the state-owned BBC was formed from it, still exerting a monopoly on radio broadcasts. In the early 1930's *Radio Luxembourg* began directing transmissions towards the UK, an action which the British government condemned as 'pirating the wavelengths that the BBC used.' *Radio Luxembourg* began to regularly change the frequency at which they broadcast, frustrating the British government's attempts to shut them down.

Inspired by *Radio Luxembourg*, *Radio Mercur* began broadcasting in 1958 from a specially converted ship off the coast of Denmark. The Danish authorities labelled it 'pirate radio' because it was considered a lawless attack on the monopoly of the Danish National Broadcasting Corporation. Mercur then became the inspiration for a whole host of other pirate stations, including, beginning in March 1964, *Radio Caroline*.

Caroline is important because it provides an archetype for what pirate radio should be about. At the time, the *BBC Light Programme* was the only real outlet for non-classical music. During the working day, *Music While You Work* continuously broadcast a series of light orchestral work, dance and military band numbers. Strict BBC rules needed to be adhered to: jazz was not allowed as the music was aimed at factory workers and should be familiar, not lethargic, with an even tempo and no over-loud drumming. The aim was to make workers cheerful so they could whistle and sing along; the result was a generation of young people who felt excluded by the BBC, and had to put up with a single 4pm slot on a Sunday where their 'chart' music would be played.

Here was a monopoly that was blocking access to what a voiceless section of the population were crying out for: it is unsurprising that pirates emerged to help. *Caroline* began broadcasting pop music, and young people in their tens of thousands tuned in. The state responded in the familiar way: trying desperately to shut down the pirate stations that began to follow *Caroline's* lead, which they managed to do via the Marine Offences Act of 1967, banning offshore broadcasting. Just six weeks after the act had become law, the BBC underwent a radical overhaul, and the Light Programme became BBC Radio 2, with a new 'youth station' - Radio 1 - focusing entirely on pop music. It's first DJ was Tony Blackburn, who presented the first 'breakfast show' on the station having presented his last morning show on *Caroline* just the day before.

This relieved the pressure for some time, and provided the emerging teenage demographic to get the music that they wanted. But teenagers were just one fraction of an increasingly multicultural and multiethnic Britain, and as other groups found the airwaves blocked to their sort of music or message, they had no option but to turn to the model of *Caroline* and go pirate. The black music station *Dread Broadcasting Corporation* began broadcasting illegally in 1981, with daring kids hanging antennae off the tops of tower blocks, ready to pack up and move or hide equipment at a moment's notice. Similarly, gay radio, Asian radio, hyper-local radio all began to find voice under the radar of legal broadcasting. Publications such as the brilliantly anarchic (and shockingly typeset) *Radio Is My Bomb* (1987) were printed to help would-be pirates with everything from transmitter placement to circuit diagrams and ways to avoid police detection:

> *This is intended as a 'Do-It-Yourself' Pirate's Handbook, aimed at promoting neighbourhood, political and open-access radio pirates... But obviously you can use it as you wish.. You can build the transmitters and use them to jam out Aunty Beeb, you can play your favourite music, or you can set up local open-access stations as we suggest... Or you can set up a fascist station and we'll come and kick your heads in!*

Radio Is My Bomb came packed with stories from El Salvador, West and East Germany, Spain, Ireland, Japan, Canada, The USA, France, Belgium... The message was clear: this was a global movement of libertarians, who saw pirate radio as a way of subverting states that routinely blocked and controlled access to information.

Pirate radio, in other words, *is* pirate, through and through. Its DNA runs back through the sea-faring rebels who fought for just treatment and an equal voice, and through the book-pirates who risked so much to set information free. As we shall see later, this is a battle that is still being fought, as media companies vie with internet 'pirates' and pharmaceutical giants wade in against copy-cat producers in the Third World.

Looking back in history, and around us in the present, we see pirates rampaging on all sides. They are on the t-shirts of our children, on the screens of our cinemas. They have claimed seats in our parliaments and declared war on our computers. In the clamour to claim the right to raise the Jolly Roger, we might well wonder what the *hell* it is with pirates, and be left reeling and rum-headed, wondering quite why they have infiltrated so many areas of life. Why do we find skulls and crossed bones almost everywhere we look? Moreover, as protest movements multiply and the global economy lurches from crisis to crisis, leaving the poorest sunk and jobless and the rich bailed out and fancy-free, it seems that we actually need the pirate spirit of Roberts, Teach and Fly to rise strongly again and come to our aid. So, having sailed quickly through history and gathered this motley crew of rebels from Rome's shores to London's airwaves, we need to clear the decks a little, get our booty out of the hold and ask what the essence of this driving spirit of these true pirates was, and whether the Jolly-Roger bumper stickers and baby-grows they have given birth to are worthy descendants at all.

[*Executive Pirate Tie, £15*]

3

Captain Pouch

Defending The Commons

Beating the Bounds

In April of 1607, in a group of small villages in the Midlands of England, a tinker named John Reynolds led a series of riots which came to a head a few months later that June. Their action focused on the local landowners, and in particular one Thomas Tresham, who had become fiercely hated in the area for his enclosures of common land. By taking common land into his full private ownership he could farm it more intensively and harvest considerably more profits than he skimmed from the serfs and tenants who had previously worked it. Reynolds became known as 'Captain Pouch' because he promised in his speeches that he had the authority of the King of England and the Lord of Heaven to defeat Tresham and the others, and that he kept in his pouch a special substance that would protect the rioters from harm.

At the peak of the unrest, some 5000 villagers - women and children included - tore into fences and smashed down the enclosures. The government of the day was in a quandary, because the Tresham's were a notorious Catholic family who had been involved in the gunpowder plot to blow up parliament. Still, the peace needed keeping, so King James ordered the riots to be put down. However, the usual local militias refused to act, forcing Tresham and the other landowners to arm their own servants and send them out against the rioters. On the 8th of June things came to a head in an ugly battle in which nearly 50 people were killed. Reynolds was captured and, as was the manner of the day, hung briefly before being taken down, neck broken but still very much alive, and a deep slit made in his abdomen. His internal organs were ripped from this wound - in other words, he was 'drawn,' or disembowelled while still alive - and then his body was butchered into quarters. All that was found in his pouch was a piece of green cheese.

The Midland Revolt started in April because it was then, in the week around Ascension Day, a ritual known as 'beating the bounds' was enacted in every parish in England. Men of the clergy, as well as the local constable, labourers and the young boys of the area would march around the parish boundary, singing hymns and consuming beers and cakes provided by the village. The purpose of this march was two-fold. Firstly, it was to knock into the heads of local people the extent of the parish's lands, so that - in the days before maps were widely available - this important knowledge was passed from generation to generation. Secondly, the march was made to ensure that no fences or enclosures to the common land had been erected. Any that were found were ripped up and beaten down. Access to the commons was a right since time immemorial and where this access was blocked, men would rise up to trample down what lay in their path. That fateful April in 1607, the ritual of beating the bounds led by Pouch escalated into a bloody massacre. The issue of enclosure had become one of the most explosive political issues of the day. To the local people in the villages that had traditionally used this land, these fences could mean the difference between life and death, because removing their access to common land prevented them from growing crops. With no income to be able to buy the grain that the newly enclosed farms produced, the people faced destitution and starvation.

In pre-Norman England almost all of the land was worked in common. Communities would toil and harvest together, sharing in whatever they reaped. After the Norman conquests much of this land gradually became associated with a local manor, and the lord who lived there. Common rights to the land were still granted however, but these came in return for service - military or otherwise - should he need it. These were 'feudal commons' and were oppressive, a far cry from more ancient and idyllic models of common agriculture, but they at least gave each person some rights of access. A common farmer would have the right to cut rushes, but perhaps only between Christmas and early February, or the right to cut wood, but only up to a certain height, and only that which could be carried on one's back.

So, despite the oppression of the lord of the manor, the commons - the woods and fields - still functioned, as Lewis Hyde has put it, 'like a theatre within which the life of the community was enacted.'[1]

The feudal landlords were not liked, but what Tresham and others were doing were finally and more completely expelling the community from the common land they had existed on for centuries, and doing so for profit. The communal theatre had suffered gradual erosion due to 'enclosure' of common land since the 1200's, but in Tresham's time enclosures were accelerating. This was not universally popular with the government of the time, who saw that villagers who had lost their common lands - and thus their properties too - were turned into vagrants. Vagrants were classed as criminals and treated as such too. Landless and homeless, they were seen as a threat to law and order, and Tudor governments passed legislation to stop the enclosures that were turning villagers into seditious vagabonds.

Yet Captain Pouch and other 'levellers' - the later movement taking its name from the hedge-levelling Midland's Revolt - were fighting a losing battle against a landed class who wanted to increase their wealth. By the end of the 19th Century the enclosure of England's common lands was almost complete, leaving just a few heaths and village greens in common ownership. So easily abstracted and glossed over as history, Hyde uncovers the personal pain of this process in the 1812 enclosure of Delaware Forest, in Cheshire. As an appeasement, half of the land went to the King. All rights to common use of the forest - woodcutting, coppicing, hunting and peat cutting - were withdrawn. The previous landowners were given other plots of land. The tenants of these landowners - the farmers who actually worked the land and had enjoyed ancient 'estover' rights - the use of land to grow food and chop wood enough to sustain his family - were meant to receive financial compensation, but were given nothing. As Hyde notes, 'such [an enclosure] severs the land, the users, and the use rights, commodifying the first and last of these and leaving the middle term - the human being who once used the forest - changed from a commoner into a modern cash-economy individual.'[2] And here we see the link - the removal of the commons is not simply about being able to walk freely for leisure, it is again about a radically altered wage-relation, one that pirates fought to wrestle back into their control. Losing their access to common land meant having to submit to a capitalist idea of labour, from which someone else would make their profits. It was a profound change, and, given the wide levels of protest we are seeing around the world against corporate greed, one that we are perhaps still suffering the cultural, economic, social and psychological after-shocks from. For these commoners, their alienation from the ground that they were born on, played on, planted in, harvested from and were buried in, was complete. Adam, drawn from the clay, had been finally ripped from his roots.

Pencil Despots

We are this new Adam's descendants, and thus the idea of the commons - once so central to so much of what it meant to be human - is now somehow strange to us. More than that, at the end of the 20th Century the common- prefix has become a taboo in much of the west with the demonization of Communism. The idea that the central core of our labour, sustenance, leisure and social life should be based around a space that was outside the bounds of private ownership, which we had to share with others, is so foreign now. But we are exception rather than the norm, for life centred on a commons has been the default human way for thousands of years across virtually every culture.

The wrench away from this, the move to enclose and make private what was once in common ownership and shared by all, has reached into every part of our lives. It took the land we once worked together, and stories we once passed to our children. It took the music we once danced to, recorded it and etched it onto a disc, to be heard only when paid for. It took the links we once walked, now mowed and sculpted to within an inch of their lives, to be driven over in buggies only by those with money enough for memberships and green fees. If the commons was the theatre in which the life of the community was played out, it is only in the past hundred years that we have seen that stage reduced into a tiny living room behind a locked front door with space only for a nuclear family, a television, and piles of commodities, things we have bought in the vain hope that the ache of our separation will be dulled.

The things we buy do dull the ache, but only for a short time. Once the new devices and clothes have been unboxed and hung in wardrobes and connected to networks, the ache returns again, and it does so because it originates in the human history of shared existence and common ownership which far precedes the modern idea of private property. Hidden beneath our heavily enclosed world, with its high fences, encrypted DVDs and lengthy copyrights, there still hangs over an ancient sense within us that our lives shine most brightly when shared with the lives of others, and become most meaningful in the spaces beyond the objects we consume behind closed doors.

Lewis Hyde discusses what we mean by 'property' and takes us back to the original sense of 'right of action.' In other words, if I own something, I have certain rights to do what I like with it. For example, if I buy a pencil then I am its despot: I have an unbounded right of action over it, and can do with it exactly as I please: draw with it, break it, sharpen it, chew it. But many other 'properties' I can buy come with more limited 'rights of action.' To take the example of a house, in the US it may not be on the National Register of Historic Places (which, interestingly, brings little *duty* of preservation, just a *tax break* if you do... a policy nudge that says a great deal in this context) but, even though I may do many things to it, I cannot, as Hyde points out, 'put a herd of cows in my yard; I cannot convert my home into a soap factory; I cannot build a tower ten stories high; I cannot even rent an office to a friend, for I live in a non-commercial zone.'[3]

In other words, owning a property, even in the US, does not bring with it fully despotic rights of action. When planning what we do to our properties, we are obliged to think about our neighbours, because our homes, however secluded, are built on the same land, the same earth. However reduced, there is still a sense of the commons here, which we can define as 'a property in which more than one person has rights.'

When these multiple rights are reduced, communities are impacted: the stage upon which the theatre of their shared lives in enacted is narrowed. In the case of the land in England, this enclosure of the commons into private ownership was almost always done for profit. Rather than allowing multiple parties to engage in activity on a shared basis, land was enclosed to make it produce more efficiently, which had the double result of forcefully turning small-scale producers with some rights to sow and reap on the land, into consumers who now had to purchase what it produced. This enclosure was really the end of a long process by which the powerful removed the community from the land they had once held in common. First the feudal lords of Norman times gave tenants and serfs limited rights to produce (though it would be incorrect to say that these lords should be seen as despotic owners, as they knew that they couldn't change use-rights without common consensus). Much later - through acts of parliament, they finally took the land entirely for themselves.

The commons was taken into private ownership, and thus became 'blocked.' By this I mean that the ancient rights of access to it and action upon it were changed, and the poor who had for generations been allowed to make use of these lands were now blocked from doing so. Moreover, this blocking was done by the lords for financial gain. The land that once provided for all was worked more intensively and, with the introduction of more agricultural technology, with less manpower. The landowner was thus able, like Willy Wonka behind his closed factory doors, to create great wealth for himself, and harvest a rich profit from land now hidden behind high hedges.[4]

But this blockage of the commons did not just create antagonism between the poor and the rich. The financial questions were part of a wider grievance about having lost the land itself, land that was the wide theatre of their ancestors, the deep stage of their past. Losing this connection to the earth meant losing part of their humanity. And as the lands were cleared and the poor drifted from the hills into the factories, their industrialised labour now part of the great machine of capitalism, something about being human, about living in rich integration and dependence on the earth, wilted and died.

Unblocking the Commons

Or, at least, withered. For this ancient and perhaps romantic ideal of living freely, of working for no one but one another, of sharing in the bumper harvest and helping one another through the hard times, lived on in the hopes and dreams of the vast lower classes. Captain Pouch led the Midland Revolt against Tresham's enclosures, but his title and spirit would have seen him warmly welcomed a century later offshore into that last great commons of the earth - the ocean.

In 1607, as the fields of England were progressively hedged off, there still remained far off lands beyond the horizon where the plains were so vast that no one could thinkably own it all. There were distant shores in abundance, lands flowing with milk and honey. Yet over the next hundred and fifty years a huge battle ensued between England, Holland, France and Spain for control of these enormous, apparently virginal commons. They used mostly African slave labour to work these new lands, and the labourers they worked to enforce and extend the traffic around these new international enclosures were the sailors on the merchant and navy vessels.

Once these maritime labourers saw, like Pouch, saw that they were to be equally disenfranchised from this new world as they had been from the old, they rose up. Pouch was a nuisance in one county; these sailors were 'villains of all nations,' but they were all pirates with a common mission to beat down the enclosures, defend the commons, and fight to unblock access to the materials and places that were the theatre of their existence. As Spring turned and each local parish church celebrated the resurrected Jesus' ascension into heavenly splendour, the poor and the pirates also rose up from the dead lives the rich had predestined for them and fought off the enclosing of wealth into privatised farms and splendid palaces.

This, then, is what we can take 'pirate' to mean: one who emerges to defend the commons wherever homes, cultures or economies become 'blocked' by the rich. Be it land that is being enclosed, or monopolies that are excluding and censoring, or wealth that has been hoarded, blockages to what should be shared freely and equitably create the conditions in which pirates will be found. Moreover, as we have seen and will see from the many pirates lurking in these pages, we can conclude that when they rise up, they tend to do so from places of poverty and need, partly because it is the poor and needy who feel the effects of enclosure more immediately and more profoundly, and partly because it is the poor and needy who tend to be bonded in labour to service these enclosures where they are found. As we will also see, wherever pirates emerge they are vilified as 'the very negation of social order' by the powers that be - whether that be the British Navy or the Lords who own the land - and their resistance branded as common thievery and thuggery. As such, they are, in every case, dealt with brutally and violently. Protests are not just broken up, but met with savage force. Men are not just arrested, but publicly hung drawn and quartered. Draconian legislation is passed to fight them, and international forces throw their might together against them.

Yet pirates, being poor and used to oppression, know their lot, and are pragmatic about their fate. They know that they are not well-educated revolutionaries, drawn from a wealthy disenfranchised political class who are out to overthrow those in power and seize control themselves. Pirates know their place, and know that full-scale revolution is beyond them. This is what makes them even more dangerous, because they refuse to organise politically or challenge the status quo through careful military campaigns and parliamentary debates. Why? Because they know that the law and the might of the Empire will either prevail against them, or seduce their leaders into suitable compromises. The pirate's vision is, in a way, very simple: they see where access to a commons has been blocked, and they work to unblock it. They see things that are not equitably shared that once were, and fight to restore some parity.

We can see this key work of unblocking in the other pirates we have already met too. In the case of Henry Hill, the book pirate, he made it very clear that he was resisting the monopoly on publishing that the Guild of Printers and the Crown had created. As early as 1712, the British government was imposing 'stamp duties' on newspapers and news-sheets. These rose steadily until, a century or so later, the price of a newspaper had risen to hit the typical daily wage of a typical earner - around 6*d*. The 'enclosing' of books and newspapers as expensive items prevented the knowledge they contained being freely available to anyone but the most wealthy. The blocking of free speech in the highly censored environment that the Crown insisted on in return for publishing privileges prevented the free movement of radical ideas, and thus choked innovation and democratic accountability. 'Publishing monopolies,' wrote John Locke, were designed to 'let Mother Church remain undisturbed in her opinions.'[5] Only the wealthy could be part of the informed public. Enlightened thought was enclosed.

Hill can thus be called pirate as much as Pouch and Blackbeard. Pouch considered the land to be a gift from God, which all should have equal access to benefit from. Blackbeard and his fellow pirates considered it a grave injustice that sailors on royally chartered ships were bonded labourers, taking resources from the commons of the new world for the sole benefit of the King and a few selected merchants. For Hill, human knowledge was as much a part of the commons as the fields of England or the far shores of the Caribbean - and, as all pirates do, he paid the price: his printing presses were not just removed, but smashed to pieces.

We can see the blockages in radio broadcasting too: the music that a huge demographic wanted to hear simply could *not* be heard easily on the BBC. They had the time and technology to play 'pop', but appear to have thought it indecorous, and unsuitable for hot-collared working men and women to listen to in factories during the day. A couple of hours on a Friday night, yes, but anything more would be... *distasteful*. The BBC's policy amounted to grand snobbery: they knew what people ought to listen to, what *real* culture was. They had the monopoly, granted by the government, and so they would only play what was respectable. This had a double impact, the reduced income from limited airplay blocking bands' abilities to pursue their creative direction, and the limited audience throttling the popularity of new music. The institution of the government-backed BBC was thus able to both stifle the growth of the artists creatively (and therefore trash what they were producing as unprofessional) and minimise the audiences they got (so they could argue that demand was low.) This sort of double-blockage worked in later struggles too, with black and gay radio emerging first on pirate stations both because the mainstream stations didn't want the message get to be heard, nor did they want the people carrying it to develop their ideas. This was not so much an enclosure of a musical commons, but an attempt to prevent the spirit and values of these radical new movements - pop, black, and gay radio - from entering the commons at all. So long as these ideas could be marginalised, they could be controlled.

We can now say that 'pirate' radio stations really *were* pirate, as they performed a work of unblocking on behalf of the marginalised. Yet what of the pirates of Puntland? Here the story is slightly more complex. What is clear is that we are - in the original wave of pirate activity, rather than the latter waves of gang-organised criminality - looking at a very marginalised community. Here are fishermen whose livelihood has literally been poisoned. What subsistence Somali fishermen saw was their commons - the fish in their oceans - being stripped and spoiled by industrial Western trawlers. Having seen the livelihood that had sustained them and their ancestors for generations completely broken, they were forced to look to other means of survival. Here were ships serving the same masters that emptied their seas, now sailing past without a second glance, carrying billions of dollars of goods. The actions of the pirates of Puntland speak loud and clear: you have destroyed the commons of our fishing waters without a second thought for us - and now you flout before us, locked up in containers, flashy goods you have bought with the money you made. Somali piracy is thus not direct an unblocking of the commons, but a distress flare sent up both in grief for a commons that has been lost, an angry broadside shot across the bows of a blocked capitalism that has ridden rough-shod over these desperately poor people.

Have-A-Go Heroes

What makes pirates so frightening to the powerful is precisely their lack of orthodoxy, their total lack of class and their lack of education. Theirs is an entirely different set of beliefs, based on liberties that reek of heresy. Rather than challenge them to a fair fight like good revolutionaries should, pirates raise two fingers to the whole charade. The root of the word pirate is the Greek word 'peira', which roughly translates as an 'attempt' or 'assault.' In other words, they were going 'to have a go.' They'll chance it, because they can hardly lose. They know their place: death will be upon them if they fight or if they stay; if life is going to be short, it may as well be merry.

This petrifies those in power because the laws that they have so carefully constructed to keep everyone in their right place fall utterly flat. Pirates have no fear of being caught and no fear of punishment because they have already been punished enough: the law carries no deterrent when applied to those who have already suffered everything. Instead, knowing that their time is short, pirates throw themselves with an extraordinary verve into life and all its fullness. The pirate radio stations around London's council estates were edgy, chaotic and sometimes utterly brilliant because the DJs who ran them knew that at any time the antenna might be spotted, the equipment have to be hidden and their records quickly moved. Every track a DJ selected was potentially their last. The pirate printers who produced pamphlets and news-sheets, seditious editions and downmarket copies, knew that they had to work fast, for soldiers might be at the door any moment, ready to smash their presses and seize their fonts. Their publications had to be cheap for the word to reach the common man; there was little point trying to raise prices when you knew you wouldn't be around to benefit from any profits. The pirates of the early 18th Century *did* lead a wild life, drinking and reeling and making merry, for they knew that at any time they could be seized and made to perform their dance 'to the four winds', as hanging was known.

Pirates show a pragmatism about their status. They suffer terrible oppression, but the fight that they put up is not designed to overthrow the powerful. They know that this is beyond them. Rather, by their short and merry uprisings, by the Temporary Autonomous Zones that they create, these small bubbles of radical freedom, they hope to enjoy their time while they can. Their campaigns for change are not coordinated or calculated, and may be limited to a speeches such as Fly's as he stood on the gallows, lashing out at those who trod on him.

His was not a speech of a revolutionary fighting to change the system by force, but the resigned last shout of a pirate who had lived out a changed life, who had, as Gandhi put it centuries later, become the change he wanted to see. This modelling of a different way - functioning democratically, sharing spoils equitably and living according to a code - was not a carefully thought out strategy designed to bring down a regime. Instead, it was the modest tactic of a group of men fed up with their lot, and committed, for the short time they had left, to exercise their own liberty in the small spaces that they created. Pirates did not overthrown their Captains in order to become despots themselves. Theirs was not a fight *for* power as much as an attempt to fight *against* power.[6]

Jolly Roger

Pirates emerge to 'unblock the commons,' but they do so with the tactic of TAZ. Their actions are temporary, and they are imperfect. Unschooled in politics or the inner workings of the law, they don't pretend that they are waging a careful campaign of change such as Wilberforce did 100 years later to bring about the Slave Trade Act of 1807. He was the son of a wealthy merchant, grandson of a man who had made the family fortune in maritime trade. With a different grandfather in a different position on a different ship, he might have been of pirate stock, but Wilberforce had the education and means to work change from the inside. The sailors his grandfather would have worked with would have seen the same awful conditions that later led Wilberforce to fight for equal rights for slaves, but, beaten and abused, death stalking them at each turn, they had no way of making their voices heard. Yet, rather than go quietly, they raised their songs anyway, and sang bawdy and loud, even as the shadows of the gallows fell on them. 'I do heartily repent!' one pirate said as he faced the crowds gathered for his hanging, 'I repent that I had not done more mischief, and that we did not cut the throats of them that took us, and [turning to the officials around him] I am extremely sorry that you ain't hanged as well as we.'

This laughter and song in the face of death was central to the Atlantic pirates' take on life - so central that it was the very mark that they sailed under. The Jolly Roger has been simplified over the years to a skull and crossed bones or swords: traditionally it showed a full skeleton holding a dagger piercing a bleeding heart in one hand, and an hourglass in the other, and would have been stitched by pirates themselves and raised following the overthrow of a brutal captain. The symbolism is, on the surface, straight-forward and borrowed from the popular 'morbid' art of the day. All of it is visible in Christian iconography, where the skeleton represents mortality, the sword the transitory nature of life, and the hourglass the unstoppable passing of time and inevitable march of fate. Yet closer inspection reveals some revealing changes. In the Christian version, the skull would have been given a small pair of wings, signifying how the soul of the departed was to be flown off to heaven and into peace. In the pirate version there are no wings. There is no flight to paradise.

For all sailors the skull and crossed bones was a familiar ensign. It was entered into the ship's log when a member of the crew died, and given the frequency of death on board, this would have peppered the pages regularly. We have seen how sailors were brutalised by tyrannical officers. Often forced into going to sea, they were, as we have heard from the testimony of a surgeon of the day, 'caught in a machine from which there was no escape, bar desertion, incapacitation, or death.'[7] The raising of the Jolly Roger was thus deeply significant. It represented the pirates' embracing of their fate - they were going to die - and yet their resistance of death at the hands of their despotic masters. Their skulls had no wings. They were going to die, but not just yet, and certainly not at the behest, nor in the name of the 'Christian' religion that their captains preached.

In the 18th Century, 'Old Roger' was a common name for the devil; to name their flag the *Jolly* Roger was to embrace a merry devil, and dance with him. It is important to understand just how deeply engrained the Christian religion was in Western life at this time, and just how completely pirates spat into the face of it. Orthodox Christianity of the 17th and 18th centuries was experienced by the masses as little more than a form of social control. There were radical Christian sects like the Anabaptists who preached about a Jesus who had sided with the poor and vociferously criticised the corrupt merchants, but this was a long way from the rituals deadened by almost compulsory attendance in the mainstream churches which reinforced the status quo, with God looking kindly on the rich and powerful and a promise of riches in heaven for the poor who knew their place and behaved well. In this sense, the Christian faith had become blocked: enclosed around the private interests of the wealthy rather than an open space in which, as St Paul had written in one of his letters, there was 'neither slave nor free, Jew nor Greek, male nor female.' Pirates, unsurprisingly, utterly rejected this form of religion, and their adoption of the Jolly Roger, with its corrupted Christian symbolism, is a clear sign of that. But, as we have seen in the legend of Captain Mission and the Italian priest Caraccioli, there is some evidence that pirates 'unblocked' this dead orthodoxy and lived out a gospel of social inclusion that appears, on the surface, to be far closer to the message of Jesus than that which they had heard from the pulpit.

Others challenged religious authority and cultural norms on land, but part of what made the pirates so despised was their position as sailors. The ocean was a place to be feared, from whence monsters, invaders, disasters and strange things came. By living at sea pirates had rejected the social virtues of church attendance and stable family, by rebelling against the masters they had also rejected 'honest labour;' by rejecting allegiance to any nation they completed their damnation. They were thus, in the pompous eyes of the patriotic religious, 'stripped of all human characteristics... a wild fragment of nature that could be tamed only by death.'[8]

Beautifully distilled into this flag then is the whole of the pirate spirit. They knew death was their fate, but they would dance for a while anyway. By raising this black standard the ships they approached understood that here were opponents who did not fear God, nor even death itself. The Jolly Roger was doubtless designed to inspire fear and supplication in the hearts of those they attacked, but there is something more profound and heartfelt in its symbolism. The skull and crossed bones does not just mean 'we are bringing you death'; rather it announces 'we are the dead.' We, the shat-on, the abused, the flogged, the ones you treated as less than human, have escaped your power, have slipped away from the identity you foisted onto us. We, the ones who you took for dead, are returning *as the dead* – and thus free of all fear, free of all human labels or classifications or ranks. We might say that pirates did not raise the Jolly Roger as a symbol of violence, but rather as a declaration that *no more violence could be done to them*. They were dead, and yet lived still – and thus the Empire should tremble in fear, for the powerless slaves it had thought could only be tamed by death, had gone beyond death and were free and living without fear of God, the law, or any majesty of any nation.

In the eyes of the state and of the church pirates were, as Cotton Mather - perhaps the most intransigent and famous cleric in the Americas at the time - wrote in 1726, 'guilty of all sins,' and had 'banished every social virtue.' As Rediker comments, 'the pirate's enemies had slowly but thoroughly disconnected him from the social order, showing him to be the enemy of all individuals, property owners, the colony, the empire, the King, the British nation, the world of nations, and all mankind.'[9] Cast out from all civil society, they were marked down as dead already. And yet they lived still.

Captain Pouch's rioters predated the Atlantic pirates by a century, but in their resistance to the enclosure of the commons we see the same principles at work. Removed from the land these tenants and serfs were now mere vagrants - and thus by their very status - or total lack of it - considered criminal by Elizabethan England. With no way of supporting themselves they were as good as dead, and with no status they had no voice with which to put their case. Their riots may not be very merry, but the fear they inspired in the landed gentry was precisely the same fear that naval captains experienced in the Caribbean: opponents who, having been shafted by the law and left for dead, feared neither death nor the law.

It is this fearlessness in the face of structures that have oppressed and marginalised them that marks pirates out, whether they be broadcasters, book-binders, sailors or serfs. 'Whatever you fear,' Rediker writes as he describes the spirit in which pirates sailed under the Jolly Roger, 'whether violence, destruction, the devil, death - we are that. We embrace it. We are the other. You have made us ugly, and we throw that ugliness in your face.' Drawing together what this extraordinarily powerful flag meant, he concludes that it serves to sum up piracy altogether: 'a defiance of death.'[10]

Bare Bones and Zombies

The Jolly Roger, with its full skeleton, was thus a potent emblem of pirates complex relationship with death. Many sailors turned pirate in order to avoid the brutal treatment that would have brought death to so many of their fellow crew, and yet those who did knew that the gallows would stalk them. Perhaps the difference between those who chose to bear the suffering of life aboard a naval ship and those who rebelled boiled down to a difference in their respective beliefs about death. The sailor who suffered in silence, who refused mutiny, perhaps did so believing the Christian narrative of their oppressors: that remaining law-abiding and dutiful would see them rewarded in heaven. Those who turned pirate perhaps did so because they no longer believed in this paradise-to-come. If this life was all that there was, they weren't about to hang around in abject poverty on the off-chance that riches awaited them once they died. They needed to live for the now. Once death came, there would be no winged-skull to take them elsewhere. The flightless skeleton of the Jolly Roger carried not simply a message of death, but of the bodily decay that followed, leaving nothing but bare bones.

The subconscious message of the Jolly Roger is thus not just about 'becoming the dead' but a statement about what happens when a body dies. The Christian understanding of paradise was - and still mostly is - as a place where those who are good experience a bodily resurrection and enjoy life eternal. Death is therefore a suspension of animation, and, as this, can be preached as something rather beautiful and heroic. Christ's death on the cross is represented as painful, yes, but comes with the glow of his complete restoration just three days later - a period he spent, if John's gospel is to be believed, as cadaver preserved and spiced with seventy-five pounds of myrrh and aloes. This is not just a Judeo-Christian aspiration. In many other religions we see attempts at bodily preservation, in the hope that it can survive the move from earthly death and on into heaven beyond.

The embalmed corpse stands as a symbol of resistance to death, but, more importantly, to the decay that follows. If the perfectly-preserved Christ is the model for the body that has made the round-trip to heaven and back, then the oozing, slowly decaying zombie is the archetypal image of the resurrected body that has remained on earth. In Haitian and West African religions, zombies are reanimated corpses, brought back to life by mystical means. Quite how they made the transition from these religious figures into their current fictional state as flesh-hungry tyrants remains unclear, though the title of George A. Romero's influential *Night of the Living Dead* makes the point clearly enough: zombies are those who have died on earth and yet remain living. Not dead enough to rest in peace, they are neither alive enough to sustain their bodies - which are almost always shown in some state of decay - and must attack the living in order to survive.

Scenes of decomposition are reflexively revolting to us. Mouldy food, the stench of decaying organic matter, flies and maggots and vultures: whereas death can be cold and hauntingly beautiful, the process of decay that follows is met with universal disgust. The reasons for this may be many, but one is certainly the subconscious recognition that the decaying body is a body that has truly lost. Not only has it died, but it is unable to transition into paradise and, rather than holding on to its form, is being dismantled and returned to the earth. In Christian theology Jesus is sometimes described as the 'second Adam' - rising above and transcending the earthy mud from which Adam was formed in the opening of the book of Genesis when God's breath was breathed into him. If this is so, then zombies are very much Adam unreformed: the divine breath in him totally exhausted, a living-dead, decaying body returning to the clay from which it came.

From a religious viewpoint, the decay of the body that has died is a mark of earthy godlessness. But from a biological perspective, it is precisely the move from death to decay that is at the heart of all living ecosystems. At the plant level, without organic decomposers like bacteria and fungi breaking down and decaying dead organic matter, vital nutrients would be trapped and never be released back into the soil. This would mean that plants would be unable to grow and, because plants are at the base of every food chain, every ecosystem would collapse: the cycle of life would grind to a halt. There have been periods in history where this has (partially) been the case. In the carboniferous period, large quantities of wood were buried and not broken down because the bacteria and insects that could effectively digest them had not yet evolved. These fallen trees were laid down as coal deposits, dark and cold and undying.

Without the process of decay we would literally be climbing over dead bodies. Death comes to all of us, but it only turns full circle and funds the next part of the cycle of life if that is followed by decay. If it is not, then the dead body becomes a vault, a hoard of vital nutrients and minerals locked up and... enclosed.

The Christian image of the resurrected and preserved body can thus be connected to the 'blocked' and enclosed wealth of the powerful merchants and princes. In the art of the day Jesus' body is commonly represented - even when on the cross - as almost glowing as if embalmed. This is not a body that shows any signs of decay, and as such, it has been removed from the normal cycles of life. The priests who presided over worship of this body were clear: the church was intimately connected to the state and the monarchy, and though the church enacted a ritual of communion - where each shared in the (definitely not decomposed) body of Christ - it stood to preserve class boundaries and social structures, and did little either to encourage the wealthy to share their riches, or challenge them about the economic structures that relied on cheap, subservient labour to create their wealth.

Connectedly then, the skeletal, fully decomposed corpse of the Jolly Roger tells us not just that pirates had 'become death' to these proto-capitalist hoarders, but that they embraced the body in decay too. Here were zombies - 'the dead, re-animated' - with all the horror that that brought with it. Already considered the scum of the earth by both Church and State, pirates perhaps embraced this status as something to be proud of, for they were the maggots, the agents of decay who attacked the carefully stockpiled bodies of wealth and returned it to the ground, to the commons from which it came, where its minerals could be shared and recycled.

As such, they were reviled. They were disgusting. They were shit. They were foetid and putrid like the food they had once been served. And yet, if we take the ecological metaphor seriously, somehow these pirates were sustaining the cycle of life. If such agents of decay did not exist, there would be no loop completed. The nutrients would be locked up and, with the earth not replenished, everything would lie cold, and dead. What the merchants did not appreciate then, and what bankers are being reminded of even now, is that economic systems function in much the same way as organic ones do too, requiring some equitable level of redistribution if they are to be sustainable. Without this idea of breakdown and decay, much wealth can still be created for a short time, but eventually those who are being consumed and not rewarded in order to make it will be able to give no more.

The pirate is the thief who steals from the dead, who goes in to unlock the deep freezers stuffed with rich game shot on the common. They are doing so not using the political machinery of the day, not with lawyers or parliamentary bills or grand speeches. Perhaps if they did, they would be heroes like Wilberforce, but none of that is important to them. Pirates are no more than the few from the anonymous masses of the proletariat who dared make a stand against their being driven like beasts of burden, and tried to run things their way for a while. It was this mass of nameless, faceless poor people who laboured to build the empires from which

Wilberforce could mount his heroics. They were destitute, landless, terrorised, objectified, of both sexes and all ages, and they cared nothing for politics, because politics cared nothing for them. The few who had the guts to see a life beyond the drudgery of bonded labour, who had the audacity to dream of a few months merriment, far from home, were hunted down as villains.

This was why they became heroes to the working masses: for a short time they had stuck it to the man. They had worked as guerrillas, creating bubbles of free speech or temporarily liberating strips of land. It had taken courage, yes, but they had known that their time would be brief whether they worked dutifully on the naval ships or turned pirate. With a raised finger to the captains, to the merchants and kings and politicians, they drank to the merry life, even if it were to be a short one.

Protesting Against a Blocked World

So who are we to celebrate them? Who are we to raise their standard and claim it as our own? Which of us is oppressed or beaten, nameless or enslaved? Their stories are often fascinating, and their lives full of adventure, but none of this quite yet explains *our* continued fascination with pirates, why *their* Jolly Roger appears on *our* baby-grows and skateboards, t-shirts and bumper stickers. We ourselves are not the uprooted, landless proletarians. Where are the enclosures, and where the death?

The capitalist structure of labour and wage relations that was beginning to spread in the 17th century, has now gripped the western body so entirely that it is sometimes hard to imagine how things could be any different. Indeed, the philosopher and cultural commentator Slavoj Žižek has written that it is easier for people to imagine the end of the world than to imagine an end to capitalism. What alternatives are there left? Russian communism has disintegrated, Chinese communism is going the same way - and in both cases, the poor are the ones left behind. Capitalism has won, and yet there is no victory parade. The principle that we under-sell our labour in return for a wage that allows others to profit has infected the mind so completely that it is now accepted that it is the only possible way to be, yet that acceptance comes not with hope or joy, but with a sense of dread and resignation that, somehow, some part of us has been defeated.

It has been a slow death. The past 400 years have seen a systematic erosion of all that was held 'in common'. Bar a few village ponds and the odd piece of heath, the earth we walk on has been gradually enclosed, and the shared rights that we used to hold together are now held by private owners. We have survived, yes. But our alienation from the land that we still depend on for our daily sustenance, and for the raw materials that are the building blocks of our houses, clothes and possessions has had a profound impact.

Unaware of how food is made, we start to lack any care for what ends up on our plates: rampant obesity is a disease of privatized eating.

Unaware of what goes into the clothes we wear, we allow sweatshops to prosper, and care not for the landscapes blighted by mines digging for rare earth metals to power our hungry devices.

Lifted from the earth by air-conditioned cars – privatized, enclosed transportation – we can remain ignorant of a climate that is out of control.

Sitting our children in front of advert-bloated story-telling machines, we hardly realise that the stories we were told as children now seem as distant as fairy tales, from another time and place. And as we plug in our headphones to listen to another *X-Factor* winner covering a song we can't quite place, we no longer hear the buskers on the underground, moved from their tunnels into specially branded zones.

We don't have time to think about these things anymore, because rather than spending our time living, we have to spend more time earning a living, 'working nine to five' the polite contractual joke as we do all we can to rake in what we can to pay the mortgage while we can and save what little we can for the rapidly retreating retirement that we can hardly believe will ever materialise. Work hard, we are told, and you will reap the appropriate rewards. And yet we fawn over celebrities who appear to have no honest work that can be celebrated, and cheer on sports stars who earn more in a week than we might in 10 years, for performing mostly admirably at a game we used to enjoy more when we played it on a piece of scrub land for free with a bunch of friends from school and jumpers for goal-posts. We don't have time for leisure now, because inflation has forced everything up save our salaries, all to bail out a tiny clique of money-men who bet wildly on how much debt they could sell us, and, having lost big-time, went crying to the government, threatening to pull the whole financial system down around them if their private losses couldn't be shared publicly.

Yes, the only commons we have left are the publicly-owned debts we share having bailed out the privately owned banks.

We are not brutalised, nor often beaten or left unpaid, but our lives are no less reduced, narrowed and controlled by powerful forces far beyond our control. In the words of the philosopher John Gray, 'we are forced to live as if we are free,' – and yet know deep down that our freedom to choose from a million varieties of breakfast cereal sweetens only very thinly the constant nausea we feel that somehow *this cannot be it.*

We know this cannot be it, so constantly set sail into online oceans trawling for more - more status updates, more friends, timelines constantly refreshing as we ache behind our workstations for something real, for something to *actually* happen. If religion was once the opium of the people, then social networks and the 'always on' culture of the 24 hour news cycle are the drip drip of methadone to keep us docile, titillated, flattened and poorly informed, while we dupe ourselves into believing we are more alive, more connected, more enriched and better liked. The internet has been heralded as the new great commons, and yet, given the freedom to roam wherever we like, the parts of it we chose to inhabit are controlled by a tiny number of fantastically wealthy and powerful companies, all of whom want to take the free content we upload and create and monetize it through carefully focused advertising. It is akin to the private landowners allowing the commoners back onto the land and telling them they can cultivate it for free, so long as they allow him to perpetually bombard them with patter from salesmen every time they come to tend their crops.

We are not much brutalised, no. But we are living in a world more enclosed than ever before, sharing a commons more reduced than ever before. Our land, our work, our leisure, our culture, our sports, our music, our stories, our beliefs, our ideas - all of them have suffered blockage and private enclosure. And this, I believe, is why we still raise that Jolly Roger where we can. In a blocked and almost entirely privatised world, the small emblem of the skull and crossbones is still a nod to the memory of the thought that the pirate spirit may be lives on somewhere; that, even though we have almost entirely lost the ability to imagine an concrete alternative, a more just world can exist.

We buy pirate baby-grows and read pirate baby books because we dream of our children growing up in a society where the principle of fair sharing lasts beyond the age of 6.

We skate on pirate skateboards because we still dream of beating the bounds, of riding roughshod over the public spaces that have been enclosed by private wealth.

We watch pirate movies because we still long for an ocean beyond the horizon where comrades are brave and adventure is real, and the rewards for our work are distributed equally.

These are small, mostly unconscious acts of protest. Hummed snippets from songs of defiance long forgotten. But, though small, they are not insignificant, for they speak in whispers of the spirit of justice and equality, of the desire to exercise common rights that has lain dormant, perhaps, and been muffled by the mountains of consumer goods we have harvested for ourselves as we have reaped the apparent rewards of economic growth through the capitalist miracle. And, in recent years, the chorus has grown slightly louder, and, in places, voices have erupted into full song, casting off the Mercedes and the designer goods and gathering in ecstatic and angry crowds in Tahrir Square and Zuccotti Park.

In a beautifully exotic twist, it appears that the West has been woken up to demand a more equitable world by Islamic, Arabic pirates. 'America needs its own Tahrir,' was the simple message that the campaigning magazine *AdBusters* sent to its subscribers in June 2011, beginning a trail of events that led to the 'Occupy' movement being set up, and the stark message that 'the 99%' were not going to stand around any longer helping the 1% remain rich while everyone else suffered. The Tahrir protest was itself sparked by the wave of demonstrations that swept through Tunisia, Yemen, Algeria, Libya, Jordan and Egypt following the death of Mohamed Bouazizi. Bouazizi was a street-vendor who was routinely harassed and humiliated by municipal officials. At around 10.30am on 17th December 2010, the police once again demanded a bribe from him to allow him to continue selling his wares from a small barrow. He didn't have the money, and some reports claim he was slapped and spat on by a female municipal worker. Her aides certainly beat him up, and then confiscated his scales and pushed over his cart. Bouazizi ran to the governor's office to ask for his scales to be returned - balance was all he wanted - but the governor refused to even see him. Beaten, he took a can of gasoline from a nearby petrol station, stood in the middle of traffic, shouted out in desperation 'how do you expect me to make a living?' doused himself and set himself alight, just an hour after the altercation.

To date, Bouazizi's sacrifice has led to three governments being toppled and major concessions to combat corruption and move to more equitable systems won in ten other states. The common right to sell goods to those who need them had been enclosed in an awful web of bribery and corruption. All Bouazizi wanted is summed up in his demand for the return of his scales: he wanted things fair and balanced, but the weight of the unjust demands of the powerful and wealthy crushed him. He did what he could, burned brightly for a terrible moment, and paid the bribes they demanded with his life. Yet that small act precipitated a surge of protest that no one could have anticipated.

Time Magazine's Person of the Year in 2011 was 'The Protester.' The official 2010 award went to Mark Zuckerberg, founder of Facebook, though it was Julian Assange, founder of Wikileaks who topped a readers' poll. In 2009 it was Ben Bernanke - the head of the US Federal Reserve. From bankers to networkers to information pirates to protesters... the last few years have seen a sea-change in our attitudes to those who are meant to lead us, and in our expectations of what our economic and political systems should be doing.

Though we may lack the imagination to see concrete alternatives, we feel that same pirate anguish that Roberts and Pouch and so many others did: that we should not be beaten down while others reap great rewards from our labour. We may not be paying with our lives, but we are already paying with our lifestyles. The princes and merchants and celebrity-endorsed web-sites promised us so much: more power, more freedom, more things, more wonderful holidays... yet with family time eroded, communities fractured and work overbearing their silver-tongued patter has finally begun to sound thin, for they are the only ones who have grown rich, and have done so selling off the very stage on which we used to play, together.

It is this enduring shared memory of a now far-off time when things were not entirely driven by profit, and our lives were played out in wider, more open spaces, that perhaps lingers in the pirate motifs we now see plastered on clothes, plates and cars. These yearnings for liberty, and land within which to enjoy it, were crystallised most clearly in the dreams of the early American pilgrims. It has become known as the American dream, but in truth here is a dream common to all humanity: a rich, expansive commons on which a community can journey and live life to the full. And thus it should be no surprise to us to note that it was around the shores of this New World that the battles between the empires and companies who wanted control of this commons were fought, and that central to these troubles were pirates - common men far from home who had seen a grand vision of freedom and rebelled against their brutal masters. The great irony of these battles is that the land had already been settled for around 12,000 years by Indian tribes, who initially welcomed the new settlers with gifts of food. These gifts were gratefully accepted, but Indian hospitality was soon returned with violence, aggression and theft of land, which was subsequently enclosed.

More than any other place it is within America - modern and historic - that we see the tensions between pirates and merchants, libertarians and lawyers, most clearly. And so, as we begin to consider how we might best respond to the erosion of the commons that we so painfully experience, it is to those shores, and the Jamestown Company who sought to exploit them, that we must turn to now.

[*Pirate Yo-Yo, £5.95*]

4

Captain Newport

'Something for the Common Benefit'

The Sea Venture

In July 1609, just two years after Captain Pouch was captured and killed for fighting against the enclosures, another Captain was transporting passengers to the New World, to the great new commons over the Atlantic. Yet things were not going well. Already worried that they had been separated from the convoy of eight other ships sailing to resupply the Jamestown colony in Virginia, Captain Christopher Newport spotted further trouble on the horizon: a hurricane. William Strachey, a passenger on the *Sea Venture*, wrote that:

> *'A dreadful storm and hideous began to blow from the northeast, which, swelling and roaring as it were by fits, some hours with more violence than others, at length did beat all light from Heaven...'*[1]

Newport was a very experienced mariner, and this was his third supply mission to the colonies, yet the storm that broke around him was like nothing many on board had ever seen. It 'startled and turned the blood and took down the braves of the most hardy mariner of them all,' but, more worryingly for Newport, it battered the boat so thoroughly that the *Sea Venture* began to leak. She was a new boat, of an entirely new design, and her timbers had not yet soaked and sealed. The caulking - the fibres beaten down into the joints between the wooden beams of her hull - was blasted away by the pressure of the waves and the ship turned into a sieve. Newport ordered his crew to begin pumping water out, while others were instructed to cut down the rigging and sails to lessen the impact of the wind. Luggage and ammunition were thrown overboard to lift the ship higher out of the water, and as the crew fatigued, passengers were forced to man the pumps, which were worked continuously for 'three daies perpetuall horror,' all of them 'stripped naked as men in Galleys.' Distinctions between classes and positions were abandoned. Gentlemen of the Virginia Company took their turns alongside criminals being deported, while those not at the pumps bailed with kettles and buckets.

They did not eat, nor rest, and yet they could not keep the water out. Passengers and crew equally and totally exhausted, Newport could get them to do no more and they abandoned the fight to save the vessel. The hurricane had won. Try as he might to stop them, those who had laboured together now found a common humanity, and knowing that they would soon lie in the same watery grave, enacted an ancient maritime ritual in the face of death. Disobeying his orders, and flying in the face of commands from Sir George Somers and Sir Thomas Gates - both senior officials in the Virginia Company - the rest of the passengers and crew cracked open the supplies of liquor and, discarding their differences, 'drank one to the other, taking their last leave one of the other until their more joyful and happy meeting in a more blessed world.'

Miraculously, that more blessed world appeared before them in the shape of the island of Bermuda, and Newport managed to steer the Sea Venture to be scuttled between two huge rocks on July 28th. Not one life was lost, though as Captain his troubles were only just beginning. Bermuda was known as the 'Isle of Devils' and much feared by European mariners, who knew of its reefs and difficult weather systems, so it was with great trepidation that the soaked crew and passengers escaped the *Sea Venture* and made their way ashore - still thinking, in all likelihood, that their certain death had only been delayed. The reality was completely different. As 'the tempest' subsided (for it was reading William Strachey's account that served as part of the inspiration for Shakespeare's play) it became clear that Bermuda was a sort of heaven on earth. The climate was temperate, and food available in abundance. There were hogs that had bred on the island having survived their own shipwreck some years earlier, huge tortoises and all kinds of wonderful fruit.

There was a great irony here, for many of the commoners who had set out for the Jamestown colony in Virginia had believed that they were going to a new Eden. Poets had written 'Odes to Virginia,' calling it 'earth's only paradise,' yet the truth was that Virginia was starving, stricken by disease, and on the verge of collapse. Captain

Newport and the Virginia Company officials now had a problem. Many of those aboard had been sent away from England as punishment for taking part in revolts against enclosures, and now they found themselves in the very situation they had fought for. The crew and passengers were feasting on the very life they had always dreamed of, and yet they, as good company people, still wanted to deliver new supplies - of food and manpower - to Jamestown. Meetings were held, and decisions presented: the crew and common passengers would work to build new boats, and they would continue to Jamestown. This was met with derision. Why would they swap this idyllic life of leisure and plenty for hard work to build what would effectively be their own prisons again? In Jamestown they would subjugated workers again, and once aboard the crew would again be under orders and beaten.

Newport faced mutiny. Stephan Hopkins, an educated Puritan who believed churches should be established in the New World based on consensual politics, rather than deference to royalty or state, argued that the authority of the Virginia Company, and the magistrates that sailed with it, ended once the storm had wrecked the ship. Others spoke of their landing on Bermuda as an act of God's saving grace, and that they stood above the law of Newport and the officials. Many made mutual promises not to undertake any work which would help remove them from the island, and retreated into the woods away from the shore to begin their own colony.

The reaction of Newport and the Virginia Company representatives was swift and violent. This new utopia, based on leisure and equality of status, could not be allowed to stand. The shareholders in London must get a satisfactory return on their investment. They met the resistance by hanging one of the mutineers, and executing another by firing squad - two of the earliest capital punishments in this modern history of America. Peter Linebaugh comments on the *Sea Venture* episode in The Many-Headed Hydra: Sailors, Slaves, Commoners and the History of the Revolutionary Atlantic:

> *'Confronted with resistance that proposed an alternative way of life, the officials of the Virginia Company responded by destroying the commoning option and by reasserting class discipline through labor and terror, new ways of life and death. They reorganised work and inflicted capital punishment.'*[2]

Authority was restored by violence. Status and class were re-established with a show of brutal power. Two new ships were built, and positions were restored as they sailed for Jamestown: crew and Captain, officials and workers.

Having subjugated the majority by force, the expedition set out again. Just three men remained behind, though it is unclear exactly why they were allowed to do so, nor why they were not executed for their resistance. Perhaps Newport and the Company officials thought further violence might be counterproductive. All that is recorded is that they insisted on remaining 'to erect their little common wealth with brotherly regency.' They were wise to do so. Landing in Virginia, the survivors of the Sea Venture found a community dying and starving. Corpses had been exhumed and eaten, while others had taken to eating leather boots and snakes. The mortality rates make shocking reading: a community of 535 had been reduced to only 60 in just two years. In contrast, while on Bermuda there had only been one death from natural causes in 10 months.

Newport's decision to force those shipwrecked to rebuild and push on to Virginia suggests that he put the company and its profits before any other considerations. Though they landed by chance on a bountiful paradise, the poor passengers he had on board could not be allowed to settle. They were needed in order to make Jamestown viable and profitable. We cannot underestimate the tough decision he had to make. It could be said that he chose profits over paradise, and so, against their will and with the threat of the gun behind them, the poor were forced to work to build the means of their own re-enslavement. Or it could be said that he chose to attempt to save the people of Jamestown, and spurred his crew and passengers on to hard work in order to achieve this. Those on the *Sea Venture* had been through hell and had happened upon plenty, but by allowing his crew and passengers to remain in the Eden of Bermuda, Newport was potentially endangering the lives of the community in Jamestown who were awaiting new supplies. Yet most of those supplies were now sunk, and bringing more people to the community would only put a greater burden on Jamestown's already meagre resources. Newport, we must remember, was also in the pay of the Virginia Company, and would face huge personal sanctions, including accusations of piracy, if he refused to fulfil his contract. The shareholders and officials were powerful people that he could ill afford to anger. He was left with the same terrible conundrum that now faces us all: work hard to keep an essentially unfair economic system pumped up in order to sustain those left starving by that system, or withdraw to a better life, and put other lives with fewer choices at risk.

For most of us, the decisions we take in the face of these dilemmas have apparently little impact on the grand scheme of things. Although he would not have known it at the time, Newport's decision to go to Jamestown's rescue may have profoundly altered the course of American - and thus world - history. Had Jamestown failed, the entire project in the New World may have taken a radically different direction. Newport made it and Jamestown was eventually resupplied; its survival in the face of these trials became part of the founding myth of a nation that has remained fiercely protective of its tough-guy, wilderness image.

The Original Pirate Nation

Ironically, the America that formed from that fledgling outpost went on to embrace mutiny almost as a national policy. Newport and the Virginia Company officials fought down a mutiny on Bermuda in order to sustain the Jamestown colony. Yet, the America that grew out of Jamestown came to be seen by Europe as just as mutinous and insubordinate as the poor passengers on the *Sea Venture* who had had to be beaten back into line. Those poor slaves, convicts and adventurers had rebelled and lost; the America that emerged from the ashes of their mutiny grew in confidence and spirit, fought against the imperialism of the English and the laws that placed burdensome taxes on them, and won. Thus freed from English rule, they set about pirating anything they could from English life. Books that were under copyright in England were published freely in America. Inventions that were protected by patent in England were shipped over and copied freely.

Benjamin Franklin, born around 100 years after the *Sea Venture* reached Jamestown, was the true Founding Father in this respect. As an inventor, scientist, politician, musician, printer, diplomat and author he, in one man, stood for everything that America was aiming to be. In many ways the story of the *Sea Venture* is a brilliant founding myth, for it repeatedly presents America with the conundrum of whether to turn inwards for the benefit of the few, or outwards for the benefit of others. Franklin's life stands as a testament to turning outwards, as the story of two of his most famous inventions shows. Having done pioneering work on electricity, Franklin went on to invent the lightening conductor. But far from trying to protect his invention and patent it for his own gain, he simply published instructions on how to make one, leaving his name entirely absent. In his own words, he simply wanted to 'produce something for the common Benefit.' His new design for a Pennsylvania fireplace was similarly an amalgam of other designs he had come across. His genius was in their new combination, not in some unique invention.

The popular view of Franklin is that he was a genius, someone who thought entirely new thoughts with no external agency. As Ralph Waldo Emerson wrote of him in 'Essays and English Traits':

'Where is the master who could have instructed Franklin, or Washington, or Bacon, or Newton? Every great man is an unique... If anybody will tell me whom the great man imitates in the original crisis when he performs a great act, I will tell him who else than himself can teach him.'[3]

Yet Franklin would have utterly resisted this view. He saw his work as drawing together the work of others, of seeing new things, but only because he had the fortune to gather so much work that others had already done. As Lewis Hyde notes, 'his is not the genius of the untutored "unique" but of the commoner who seeks and absorbs the wisdom of many masters.'[4]

It is this attitude, the breaking down of enclosures that other nations had put up, the ability to synthesise and build on what others had done, that made America great in the first instance. He refused to take monopoly privileges on his inventions because he knew that he debt to others was too great. 'As we enjoy great Advantages from the Inventions of Others,' he said, 'we should be glad of an Opportunity to serve others by any Invention of ours, and this we should do freely and generously.'

Thus America grew strong by borrowing freely - pirating - from others, and seeing itself (perhaps myopically) as one enormous commons upon which all could grow and benefit. It was not a monarchy, but a Republic - from the Latin *res publicae* - where the things of state did not belong to a King or Queen, but to the people.

As Hyde writes, commenting on the freedom American publishers enjoyed:

'The British had to struggle for years to free the ancient authors from the Stationers' Company, but no such battle was needed in America, where cheap editions flourished from the start. Farmers came home from the plow to read Homer and Tacitus, or so the story always went. The typical brag appears in Franklin's memoirs: easy access to books has "made the common tradesmen and farmers as intelligent as most gentlemen from other countries." Nor did the law offer any rights to contemporary authors in foreign lands. The United States was a pirate nation for a hundred years, and proud of it.'[5]

If only this were still the case. Captain Newport's dilemma has turned entirely from Franklin's answer of the good of the many, to the modern capitalist approach of the good of the few. And with that renewed selfishness has come an attitude that inventors and creators are untutored geniuses, unique people who have no master. How far from Franklin's founding acts of piracy have we come when the Motion Picture of America Association, in their teaching materials on Patent and Copyright insists that 'if you haven't paid for it, you've stolen it,' thereby, by implication, criminalising their own Founding Father.

The Song Remains the Same

Perhaps the best example of this change in attitude towards invention, creativity and the ownership of ideas is in music. We are now experiencing the ageing of the first great generation of rock stars, with The Beatles, The Rolling Stones, Cliff Richard and Bob Dylan all entering senior years. With this ageing has come a debate about how long their music should be protected under copyright. Mick Jagger has been a very vocal advocate for extending copyright, and the European Union recently signalled their agreement with him by voting to extend the copyright period on sound recordings from 50 to 70 years. Jagger said in an interview with the BBC that 'obviously the record business is not what it was, so people don't earn as much as they used to. [The royalties] can extend their lives and the lives of their families who inherit their songs.'[6]

It would seem unlikely that the wolf is close to the door of the various Jagger mansions, but what of the deeper point he is trying to make? Jagger's argument is that, as creator of a song or recording, he - or his inheritors - should be able to benefit from sales of that song for 70 years, and also claim protection from other artists creating songs that are too similar to the ones he has written. This is, as Hyde would put it, the song-writer as the genius of the untutored 'unique.' And yet any cursory listening of Jagger's compositions will tell you that he is far more 'the commoner who seeks and absorbs the wisdom of many masters.' In other words, he wrote blues standards, using chord progressions and changes that were part of the great commons of blues music, and which no one could dare to 'own.'[7]

Kirby Ferguson, a New York-based filmmaker, has explored this in more depth in relation to another great band, Led Zeppelin. In his video series *Everything is a Remix*, Ferguson exposes how many many Zeppelin songs borrowed heavily from other material. For example, the opening and closing sections of 'Bring It On Home' are lifted from the Willie Dixon track of the same name. The 'Lemon Song' similarly borrows riffs - and lyrics - from Howling Wolf's 'Killing Floor.' 'Black Mountainside' is an obvious rip-off of Bert Jansch's arrangement of the traditional folk tune, Black Waterside. And so it goes on.

Importantly, none of this is abnormal. Musicians have borrowed from one another since forever, and most of Led Zeppelin's contemporaries were recording and releasing covers around this time too. (Remember, Bob Dylan's first album contained no fewer than 11 covers.) What was different in Led Zeppelin's case is that they refused to attribute their songs; they claimed it all as their own work - work that is now protected for decades under copyright.

In a similar way, Ferguson examines just how much George Lucas borrowed from a huge number of pre-existing films when he made *Star Wars*, lifting themes, images and even the famous rolling away title sequence from Westerns, Samurai movies and early Flash Gordon shows - some of it virtually frame-by-frame remakes.

Again, the point is not that he did this, because borrowing and remixing in this way is what story-tellers have done since the dawn of time. As Ferguson points out - and I am now borrowing and remixing - we become skilled creative people by becoming fluent in the language of our chosen art or craft, and part of that process of becoming skilled has always been to study and copy what has gone before. Rembrandt did it. Mozart did it. The Beatles did it. Indeed, one could argue that without this stage of copying and borrowing, nothing new would ever be created, as no one would have a proper grounding in the history and tradition of their form.

What appears to go against the spirit of this evolving process of copying, transforming and combining to create 'new' songs, films or products is that the musicians, directors and inventors of recent generations have then shut the door behind them, locked the vault and demanded that they get paid for their creations, over and over and over again. What was originally held in common - for remember that Snow White and Pinocchio were just folk tales in the public domain before Disney made their animated versions - has now been enclosed and made available only on delivery of appropriate payment.

The reason why this has become an issue for this generation is because the technology needed to make copies has become so widespread. If you were Antonia Stradivari, making incredible violins in Cremona in the late 17th Century, all you needed to do to protect your methods from being copied was secure your workshop each night and make sure you employed trustworthy apprentices. It was somewhat expected that, once your apprentice had completed their training and been entered into the appropriate guild of craftsmen, they would branch out, apply some of their own ideas on top of yours, and create something new. The problem for Jagger is that if he writes a song now, he has almost no control over who hears it once it is published because the recording can be copied bit-by-bit with no degradation. However, before we take pity on him, we need to remember that the very reason that Jagger is so wealthy is precisely because, for a short window of history, he *was* able to record his music *and* exert massive control over who heard it, because vinyl records were so hard to copy. What he is trying to do now is keep that cash-flow going, when it never existed earlier than the 1950's, and is very much struggling to exist for more recent artists now. (In fact, what we have seen in recent years is a return to the more traditional way of earning money as a musician: getting paid for performance. The one thing that cannot be copied is the live act. So we have seen bands releasing their recordings for free (or for donation) and doing a lot more with their live performances.)

In this way we can begin to see that there is a co-evolutionary relationship between media companies and file-sharing sites: each evolves in response to the activity of the other. Indeed, it could be said that piracy is actually *created* by the enclosure of the commons. Those who have traditionally had access to a commons simply continue to use it; the transgression is only created by the erection of a new, enclosing boundary.

An Act for the Encouragement of Learning

The pertinent question then arises: should *any* copyright be honoured at all? Is the piratic principle that there should be no protection for intellectual property, and no protection at all for artists who have created and recorded work? The Swedish 'Pirate Party' - who have recently won representation in the European Parliament - would argue not. What they want is reform of a copyright system that has become distorted. As their website states:

'The official aim of the copyright system has always been to find a balance in order to promote culture being created and spread. Today that balance has been completely lost, to a point where the copyright laws severely restrict the very thing they are supposed to promote.'[8]

To put it plainly: the considered approach to piracy is *not* that everything should be free, and everything should be able to be copied and shared without redress. Rather, what is needed is a resurrection of the original idea behind copyright, which, in the original US act of 1790, was 'an act for the encouragement of learning,' just as the Patent Act was designed 'to promote the progress of useful arts.'

Early in the 18th century a man called Chester Moor Hall invented the 'achromatic telescope doublet.' This was an ingenious way of combining two lenses to overcoming the problem of colour flare, which dogged optical instruments because of the way that light of different wavelengths refracted to slightly different extents. Hall was no optician, so had to contract out the making of the lenses. To protect his invention, he ordered each lens from a different optician, but, unbeknownst to him, each optician happened to then subcontract out the making to the same third optician. Cleverly, this optician realised what the two lenses of identical diameters would do, and so, from 1733, knowledge of the telescope doublet spread around the instrument makers of London. Although Hall never published his results the London telescope makers enjoyed a commercial advantage over other manufacturers, because they kept this new knowledge as a trade secret.

It wasn't until 1758 that, completely independently, one John Dolland, rediscovered the same telescope doublet. Rather than keep it a secret, he described and read details of his invention to the Royal Society in London, went on to manufacture lenses, and obtained a patent for his discovery. The London opticians were furious, but when the case came to trial they lost, the Lord Chief Justice decreeing that 'it was not the person who locked up his invention in his scrutoire that ought to profit for such invention, but he who brought it forth for the benefit of mankind.'

In the Justice's decision lies the founding principle of patents and copyrights: protection is given to the inventor for a limited period of time to allow them to be compensated for the time and energy and money they have invested in inventing new ideas and bring them to market. But once that limited time is up, the whole of the public domain is enhanced and others may begin to copy, transform and build upon the patented idea. Put simply, private compensation is followed by public benefit. In this way, inventors have a motivation to keep innovating, but the public domain remains enriched and renewed, and all advances end up being for the common good.

Jump forward 250 years, and this spirit of common good has been replaced by the grotesque work of patent trolls. These are companies who don't make or create anything, nor do they have any intention of making or creating anything, other than money. They buy up huge numbers of patents and let them, like Hall's telescope doublet, lie dormant. Then when others come along with similar inventions, they whip out the patent and take them to court. Legal bills being what they are, many companies simply chose to settle out of court. The trolls have their win, and crawl back under their bridge waiting to pounce on the next victim.[9]

In other words, the copyright and patent system has strayed far from its original intention of existing to promote innovation and sustain a healthy public domain. With the forces of capitalism, and the strong modern emphasis on making personal wealth, copyrights and patents have instead become a legal stranglehold on invention, which is throttling and narrowing the commons too. The laws that have grown up to support this, we shouldn't now be surprised to learn, are proposed by the rich, to benefit and protect the already-rich. Would the young and penniless Mick Jagger be fighting to enclose the blues in the same vociferous way that the old and jaded one is? The common good has been overcome by an obsession with intellectual property. Captain Newport's dilemma has been collapsed: the corporation *must* come first.

Piracy is the new Radio

In one of my favourite Simpsons episodes, as the town of Springfield approaches their bicentennial celebrations, Lisa begins to probe into the history of the town founder, Jebediah Springfield, and discovers that he was actually a notorious pirate, Hans Sprungfeld. Taking this iconoclastic discovery to the stage of the town parade, Lisa has the opportunity to inform the whole community that their hero is in fact something else, but, gazing out over the crowds gathered in their proud finery, she pulls back, and, withholding the new information, allows them to continue in their happy ignorance.

The writers of the series are often deeply subversive, and I like to think that this pulling back is a satire on the way real American history is both uncovered, and then occluded at the last moment in order to preserve a 'better' founding myth. In fact, pirates of the golden age were not so far removed from the founding fathers. Speaking on Minnesota Public Radio in 2009, Marc Nucup, curator of a piracy exhibition at the Virginia Mariners' Museum, was clear:

> *'The golden age of piracy, the early 1700s - it's not that far away from the American independence movement. [Pirates] were fighting against England and in a few years Americans would be fighting against England. It's not that hard to make a stretch between the pirates and the patriot movement. [Pirates] have always been part of the escapist fantasy that people can look to whenever they feel like their lives are too constrained.'*[10]

It was this feeling of constraint that led to many of the Puritans seeking a new life in a new land. Here were people essentially branded heretics by the English, who escaped the oppression they were under to make their own way, just as pirates themselves did. The America that evolved from these settlements was very much a developing nation, and it grew strong by playing pirate with English law - 'stealing' books and patents, and refusing to pay what the English thought they were due. With their vast and highly developed empire, the English perhaps thought that little would come of this up-start nation, other than cheap tobacco produced using even cheaper labour.

Sadly, as we have seen, this founding story of piracy has been overtaken by a litigious culture of copyright in perpetuity and violent hounding of those who dare to play pirate now. Until recently, large pharmaceutical companies in the US hounded those in new developing nations who were creating copycat versions of their drugs very cheaply. Unable to afford the hundreds of dollars for the proprietary treatments, governments in countries like India decided to turn a blind eye to companies producing 'pirated' pills that were vitally needed to improve the health of millions of their citizens. Thankfully, companies like GlaxoSmithKline have now moved to introduced tiered pricing structures to allow those from poorer nations to pay less.

This issue is far from resolved, however. Drug companies have to invest huge amounts of money in research and testing to bring new treatments to market, and thus their 'private compensation' needs are large. Yet the financial data from these corporations hardly shows them struggling to pay the bills, while many millions in desperate need of more effective drugs end up suffering as a result. America itself benefited from playing pirate as it struggled to find its feet. Perhaps America now looks at new developing countries and considers them unlikely to amount to much - other than sites for producing cheap goods with cheaper labour. Yet if the founding story of what made America great is to be believed, we should allow these other countries to play pirate too, for in gifting them a healthy public domain, huge strides in education, literacy, healthcare - and innovation - will be possible.

From my own view on the other side of the Atlantic, America's withdrawal from its piratic principles are correlated to its diminution as a place of great dreams and great freedoms. The proposed 'Stop Online Piracy Act' and 'Protect Intellectual Property Act' - on ice and being revised at the time of writing - are simply new examples of an age-old practice: the already-rich passing laws to protect their income streams by tightening and strengthening their enclosure around a commons.

In other fields there have already been big wins to take heart from. Over the past decade the sequencing of the human genome was undertaken by two separate bodies - one public, the other private. The private project - undertaken by the Celera Corporation - wanted to patent their findings and effectively place copyright control over the code for human existence. The public project - with most of the government-sponsored sequencing performed in universities and research centres in the US, the UK, Japan, France, Germany - was concerned not with profits, but the common good. A free and public release of the code would allow scientists the world over to work towards cures for diseases, without having to pay subscriptions to Celera to get the raw information first.

Thankfully, the public good won in this case. Indeed, that the human genome has remained patent-free speaks volumes about the way that life together has always evolved. The process of copying, transforming and combining is the very process that has made life, evolution and progress possible. To restrict and monetize that essential approach is to lead to evolutionary dead ends, and the slow destruction of any sort of innovative human development.

Some corporations have picked up on this principle and tried to integrate it into their philosophy. In the early days of the Mac development team, Apple had a quote stuck up around their offices: 'it's more fun to be a pirate than to join the navy.' Steve Jobs was a hard task-master - and we shouldn't pretend that he was anything other than a tough CEO who wanted to squeeze the competition and get his products made cheaply. But he did know a huge amount about the creative process, and knew that hiring 'pirates' - people who would work to remix and synthesise, rather than go for the obvious solution, was good sense.

Some musicians have also taken a different view to Jagger's. Neil Young, for one, has spoken up in favour of music piracy. When music was first broadcast over the radio, musicians reacted in a similar panicky way to those worried about file-sharing now. Many were furious about their music being played in this way, feeling that it meant that nobody would go out and buy their records. Some record labels even made their acts sign contracts saying that they would not appear on the radio. But Young is wise enough to point out: 'I look at the internet as the new radio. I look at the radio as gone. Piracy is the new radio. That's how music gets around.'[11]

Others, like the label *Records on Ribs*, have developed a model of supporting artists and raising their profile (because, isn't that sort of what a record label should be passionate about?) that allows anyone to download new music for free, and then offers them the chance to donate what they think is appropriate for it. Their manifesto is refreshingly open:

- To sell music for profit is to deny its worth. It is to reduce it to numbers, spreadsheets, targets. Desire cannot be quantified thusly.

- Tapes, CD-Rs and the Internet give us the opportunity to distribute music for free without losing significant sums of money.
- Anyone could do what we are doing. A free-for-all. Brilliance obscured by an avalanche of mundanity. There is an avalanche of mundanity already in the shops, and it costs you £9.99 a go. We only ask that you listen with open hearts and minds. And if one hundred, one thousand, one million people want to do the same as us then good luck to them. What a world that would be! A torrent of creativity freed from profit.
- We accept donations, but do not expect them. What we do costs us little, but we cannot avoid making a loss. Nor can the artists who have to buy equipment and take time to rehearse, perform and record. Any money you give us will go to loosen these burdens and will be gratefully received.

What a world away from Mick Jagger this is. This is real music, and real artistry, where people are not doing things for the money, but for the passion of creating. Jagger sees his music as a product, for which he deserves money in exchange for its use in the market. At Records for Ribs - and other similar labels - music is still held in the realm of gift, beyond the banality of market exchange value.

Does this mean that musicians should not expect to be able to make a living from their music? No, of course they should. But it may that that living needs to be re-focused on the artistry and live craft of performance. I say re-focused, for the past half century has been an exception, rather than what should be taken for a norm. It has only been in this small window that technology has existed that allowed for the tight control of the physical recording of a piece of music. It is clearly right that we have a huge amount of sympathy for the more minor artists who have suffered because of music piracy, but one cannot help but think that if the record industry hadn't done so much to exploit listeners with high prices and endless compilations and greatest hits, all supporting bloated rock 'n' roll lifestyles, then people would have felt worse about illegal downloading and copying.

Ribs for Records distribute their music under a Creative Commons licence system. It is important to understand that this is not an abandonment of copyright protection, but a realignment of it. Creative Commons licences are a way of reserving *some* rights, while still allowing the public domain to be enriched through legal sharing. For example, the Creative Commons license employed by Records for Ribs allows users to download tracks for free from their site, and to share them widely with their friends - as long as no profit is made by the user for doing so.

This helpfully boils the issue down to its fundamentals: money. The public domain, the commons, is disliked by the consumer capitalist mindset because it sees it as wasteful, as not efficiently producing money and the means to exchange commodities for profit. Yet, as Lewis Hyde has explored extensively in his brilliant book *The Gift*, the essence of life and art lies not in this market exchange, but in the exchange of gifts. What capitalism has always tried to do, whether to music or works of art or landscapes or health provision, is create a myth that the *only* way to sustain these activities is to enclose them and run them for profit.

Pirates disagree with this premise, and thus the issue of piracy strikes at the very heart of the question of what sort of nations and societies we want to be. With enclosed lands and privatised everything, a small number of us will certainly enjoy great riches and rewards. But the price of that will be a reduced public domain, a narrowed and choked stage upon which the theatre of life will be played. The alternative is one which will see fewer people reaching stratospheric wealth, but more people feeling ownership of their locality and, as economic and cultural stake-holders, enjoying the freedom to innovate and develop as a healthy commons is guarded and maintained.

Punk Pirates

As culture, style and technology evolve there has always been an interplay between the relationship music - and other arts - have with the market, with periods when the popular music of the day is highly commercial, and other times when young people have grown fed up with the state of the 'pop' industry and rebelled. What we saw with the emergence of punk in the 1970's was the most radical manifestation of this: a total rejection of the accepted norms of the day. This rejection encompassed clothing, hairstyles, the ways of making music, and attitudes to authority. Whereas the hippies of the 1960's had leaned towards the US, the punks of London's Kings Road were violently British. The Union Jack was re-appropriated in the same way that the winged skull was in the pirates' Jolly Roger: it became their fractured symbol of their zombie existence: they lived still, and were British, yet were also 'dead' to the monarchy, to the Queen and all she stood for. It is no coincidence that punk hit the big-time just as the Queen's Silver Jubilee was being celebrated.

Punk was a classic TAZ - lasting for a very short time, but in those brief moments, liberating a space and penetrating it with something marvellous. For those who experienced punk, life would never be the same again. These were not the best musicians, nor did they write the best songs, but the raw energy and 'fuck you' attitude that they displayed with such incandescence was like a forest fire, clearing away the deadened enclosed spaces of the staid music industry and creating a new commons, where anything was possible.

What is interesting is how punk has now been appropriated by young people in oppressive states throughout the world. Having been beaten down by the state for so long, what the internet has given them is access to a style of music and dress that is the uniform of radical protest and anarchy. A recent piece in The Guardian outlined this phenomenon, tracking punks down in Iraq - where the interior ministry have warned of the dangers of those who 'wear tight clothes that bear paintings of skulls and favour rings in their noses and tongues' - and to Indonesia, Russia and Burma too.[12] This is not about bands jumping on a punk bandwagon and wanting to 'make it.' These pirate-punks don't want riches for themselves. What they want is things to change. They have become disillusioned with politics, protest, religion and western intervention, all of which have failed to lift the boot of oppression from their backs.

The internet has given them access to a music that speaks into their situation. This new wave of punks are not going out to buy copies of classic punk albums, they are downloading them wherever they can get them - and one would hope that, despite the 'Great Rock and Roll Scandal' that was the Sex Pistols, Johnny Rotten would actually be pleased with them. They have taken the bricolage mentality of the *Anarchy in the UK* album cover and stitched together their own versions of the clothing and the hairstyles, appropriating what they need to serve the situations they may be in.

Though they may not be under the same direct oppression as these young people in Burma or Iraq, could it be that music pirates in the West have evolved not so much because they are selfish and unwilling to pay for music or films, but because media companies have tried to ring-fence and monetize stories and songs that have for so long be held in common? Having lost control of our traditional land and our oceans, having given away our labour to corporations who have now lost the money we had entrusted them for our pensions in speculation on money markets in places we have never visited, and having been fed endless tittle-tattle about rock star excess and Hollywood lifestyles is it any surprise at all that people have taken a somewhat free approach to music and film?

When wage negotiations are strangled by the culture of austerity that has descended after the recent banking crisis, people are naturally going to feel less inclined to listen to Mick Jagger's concerns about being paid for years and years more for songs he wrote and made millions from years and years ago. What much of the recent mood of protest has been about is the lack of a perceived principle of fairness. Bankers have continued to receive huge bonuses, despite huge losses, and it is easy to see Jagger in the same light: shouldn't he, like the rest of us, just be paid honestly for the hours he has worked? How long did it take Mick Jagger to write 'Street Fighting Man'?

> *Well now what can a poor boy do, Except to sing for a rock & roll band? // Cause in sleepy London Town there's just no place for a street fighting man, no...*

Perhaps 20 hours is a reasonable estimate. And on a generous wage of $100 per hour, plus time for recording and the cost of equipment, plus marketing and manufacturing, one might arrive at a sum of around $15,000. Many of the Stones' singles have sold well over 500,000 copies. At what point would it be fair to say that Mick Jagger has received fair reward for fair labour? Clearly, after all of these millions, he still can't get no satisfaction, and must be rewarded again and again. His music is no longer gift, no longer inhabited by some greater spirit; it is little more than a manufactured widget, reproduced and sold for profit, over and over again.

What is left of the commons is, right now, under terrible threat. But, thank God, pirates have once more emerged to defend access to what we should be able to own together. Unfortunately, the strategy of the powerful is the same as it has ever been: to chase down and violently condemn them, wherever they may be found. To label them villains of all nations, enemies of all mankind. To hang them, shoot them, imprison them and string them up as 'the very negation of imperial social order.'

There is another way. If America is to become great again, it should return to its pirate roots. Rather than fighting against pirates, it should look for the blockages and enclosures that have caused them to rise up, and use the law not to protect the wealthy, but protect and enrich the public domain. It is the only sensible thing to do, for if history has taught us anything, it is that pirates will never be defeated. On the contrary, through the inlets of the Caribbean to the Gulf of Aden and the illegal printing presses of London, through the marches around the parish boundaries to the pirate radio stations in the tower blocks and the ever-growing media-sharing platforms online, the deep-rooted spirit of freedom and equality pirates carry within them has always been passed on. It might be reduced to a cheeky skull and crossbones on a baby's stroller, a tiny graphic on a skateboard or party in fancy dress, but pirates live still, constantly trying to steer us towards equality in the face of injustice, and freedom and self-determination in the face of oppression, because this is the way life was meant to be: played out on the commons, together.

Our experience is so often otherwise. With our economies rigged towards the rich, and our arts enclosed for profit, we need these pirates to do their work in our financial districts, in our theatres, in our bookshops and public spaces. Yet we also need to them to do deeper work than this, for we know that beyond our bank balances and shared entertainments we are more than material beings.

We should be unsurprised that the degradation of the physical and cultural commons has had an impact on our inner life and our personal development too. Lives lived in enclosed environments can lead to enclosed lives. Carl Jung was not the first to realise this, but did more than any other to explore how blockages from without can lead to blockages within. He knew that large populations of people could experience corporate psychological stresses:

> *'The psyche is not always and everywhere to be found on the inner side. It is to be found on the outside in whole races or periods of history which take no account of psychic life.'*[13]

People might not have known it consciously, but the traumas of the land enclosures that whole communities experienced through the Middle Ages and beyond left profound psychological scars at the inner level too. We should not be surprised by this. Our physical environment, and the context of our labour and leisure, have a profound impact on our personal well-being. Academics such as Richard Wilkerson and Kate Pickett have shown in studies like *The Spirit Level* that the huge increases in income inequality we have seen in the past 40 years can be correlated with parallel increases in stress, obesity, depression and myriad other measures of social dysfunction. The enclosure of the material world, the endless encroaching of market-centred thinking and the belief that the pursuit of profit is the best model for a wealthy, growing society, has had a psychological cost.

Activists and writers such as Alistair McIntosh have explored this in great detail, and worked to do something about it. His extraordinary book *Soil and Soul* uncovers just how intimately intertwined our persons are with the land we inhabit, and the labour we do on it. By setting up the Isle of Eigg Trust, McIntosh began a campaign to overthrow the island's feudal landlord - helping local people to become the first Scottish community to ever to clear their laird from his own estate. He then went on to successfully campaign against a beautiful Hebridean mountain being turned into a 'super-quarry.' In playing pirate with the blocked economic and social systems, McIntosh not only charts how local people achieved material release from oppressive corporate regimes, but simultaneously achieved a reinvigoration of their inner lives too.

It is because of their integrated and holistic role that we remain so fascinated by pirates, and why they remain such important figures in our cultures and economies. The material blockages we have examined - in radio, in printing and in commerce - have had deep effects, and so it is vital, as we welcome the bawdy songs of the pirates into our public arenas, that we also look at inviting them to play pirate with our private, inner selves, and begin to move from being blocked, self-seeking consumers, to open and generous collaborators and co-creators.

[*Ralph Lauren Pirate Cufflinks, £285*]

5

Captain Hook

Unblocking the Self

Fleeing Neverland

Educated at Eton College, rising to become Blackbeard's boson, and said to be the only man Long John Silver ever feared, there was little that should have left Captain Hook afraid in battle. Yet, in the moments between finally losing his footing on the plank stretching out from the deck of his ship, the *Jolly Roger*, and entering the jaws of the crocodile in the waters below, he must have wondered quite how he had been defeated by a mere *boy*. A boy and a girl called Wendy Darling...

In 1902, a London writer released a novel which fictionalised his relationship with a group of children with whom he had become very friendly. The children's mother, Sylvia Llewelyn-Davies, lost her husband Peter to cancer shortly after, and she lasted only a few more years, leaving the author named as guardian to her children. The writer himself knew death too well: his elder brother David had died in a skating accident when he was just 13 - a tragedy that his mother never fully recovered from.

Childhood, death, and the problem of becoming parents... all of these were issues that surrounded JM Barrie when he wrote *The Little White Bird*, which introduced to the world a character called Peter Pan, a boy who would never grow up. In the expanded novel and play that came later, we find Pan darting around the upper windows of houses in Kensington. He is spotted by Wendy, and, while trying to escape, inadvertently loses his shadow.

Although the play doesn't have her name in the title it is she, not Peter Pan, who is the true protagonist, for she is the one who undergoes real changes as the narrative progresses. We are told as the play opens that it is her last night in the nursery. Wendy is on the cusp of womanhood, about to leave the locus of her childhood behind as she moves into a more adult space, and she is anxious about the transition. Yet rather than be there for her and guide her through, in the midst of this anxiety Mr and Mrs Darling leave for the evening, putting her in charge of her two younger brothers - playing mother - and it is into this scene that Pan flies in.

Hearing her stories, and picking up on her worries about leaving the nursery, he invites her to Neverland, a magical place where she need never grow up. Excited, and perhaps out of spite at her parents absence, Wendy agrees. She and her brothers fly out of the window and far away to Pan's home.

It appears to be the most wonderful life, full of adventure, with no adults to hassle them or put limits on their play. Yet it is here, ironically, that Wendy ends up again taking on the role of mother - and it is a *role* only, a *part* she must play in a very vivid game, a game that she cannot now escape. Having got to the edge of leaving the nursery, we can sense her growing frustration at having retreated to Neverland: the refuge has become a prison.

What we witness as the play unfolds is a life that is blocked. Having got to the cusp of adulthood, right to the symbolic last night of childhood, Wendy has pulled back and fled... but is now stuck. Who will come to disturb the narrative? Who can do this work of unblocking? Captain Hook, of course, and his band of pirates.

As we have heard, when people experience their lives as blocked or constrained, pirates emerge as part of the unblocking, or part of the mechanism of escape - even if just in a fantasy sense of hearing the stories about them and drawing strength from them. We know that this is true in the physical realm. We have seen how enclosures of material commons led to economic and social 'blockages,' with a wealthy elite accruing huge fortunes, at the same time excluding the very same poor labourers who worked to create the wealth. And we have seen how pirates emerge to fight these enclosures, to defend the commons, stamp down the boundaries and try to widen again the stage on which communal life can be played.

Wendy's life was no 18th century maritime trading network, nor a broadcasting or publishing monopoly, yet the problem of the blocked narrative, of her being enclosed in the permanent infancy of Neverland is solved through the familiar boom of gunfire and the roar of hearty voices, as pirates emerge to destabilise the Eden Pan has built for himself, and now trapped Wendy in.

No one can age in Neverland - even time has become blocked - so it is left to Captain Hook, his own chronological anxieties expressed in the tick-tocking crocodile who constantly pursues him, to reinvigorate the plot and lead Wendy towards personal release. Ironically, Wendy's journey to release begins with her capture by Hook. Pan comes to defend her, having battled Hook many times before, and eventually defeats him - sending him overboard into the mouth of the waiting crocodile below.

Having beaten the pirates, Wendy sees clearly that she must return home. Reunited with her mother, the play ends with Pan refusing to be adopted by the Darlings (afraid that they will 'catch him and make him a man') and Wendy making him promise that he will return for her every Spring. Spring is the symbol of rebirth, and Pan's pledge to come back each time the year renews, each time there is regeneration, echoes with hints in the play that Wendy's own mother Mary also knew him when she was younger too.

The play is thus revealed as a repeated cycle, a story of negotiating safe passage from childhood into adulthood. We see this in précis in the opening scenes, where Pan loses his shadow and needs Wendy to reattach it. In Jungian psychology interaction with 'the shadow' is integral to the process of individuation. Jung himself wrote that 'the shadow personifies everything that the subject refuses to acknowledge about himself,' so, presented as a boy who has can detach his, Pan comes to us as an archetype of childishness: refusing to engage seriously with his inner being, and thus unable to grow up. Yet this is not a story of his failure to deal with his shadow, but Wendy's success in doing so. In the traditional performance of the play, Captain Hook and Wendy's father, Mr Darling, are played by the same actor. Pan's numerous skirmishes with Hook - with the father - have taught him nothing. There is no final victor, and no movement or maturation. In contrast, the battle involving Wendy ends with the destruction of Hook. She has overcome the father, the blockage to her move into womanhood. Her struggle against the pirates empowers her to take the decision that she has so far been unable to: she must return to the 'real' world and get on with the job of growing up.

This is a significant movement in our understanding of piracy. Whether consciously or unconsciously, the story that Barrie created presents pirates as functioning not simply as agitators who can shake up a blockage in the *material* realm, but as those who can facilitate healthy disturbance at a deeper, *psychological* level too. And this is no coincidence of terms. As Jung himself wrote:

> *'As long as all goes well and psychic energy finds its application in adequate and well-regulated ways, we are disturbed by nothing from within. No uncertainty or doubt besets us, and we cannot be divided against ourselves. But no sooner are one or two of the channels of psychic activity blocked, than we are reminded of a stream that is dammed up. The current flows backwards to its source; the inner man wants something which the visible man does not want, and we are at war with ourselves.'*[1]

When things are going well, when we are developing and maturing as we should, then life 'flows' smoothly. Yet when we find our psyche 'blocked' then we become divided: parts of ourselves become enclosed against other parts, and war begins to rage. Indeed, it is only then that we discover the hidden worlds - the Neverlands and Narnias - within us. What happens then? Jung continues:

> *'Freud's psychoanalytic labours show this process in the clearest way. The very first thing he discovered was the existence of sexually perverse and criminal fantasies which at their face value are wholly incompatible with the conscious outlook of a civilized man. A person who was activated by them would be nothing less than a mutineer.'*[2]

A mutineer...

Wendy does not need to become a mutineer, a pirate, herself, for to do this she would be activating the wild unconscious desires within her thoughts in an horrific and unhelpful way. What she does instead is enter a fantasy world where she can engage pirates to begin the unblocking work that needs doing, but in a controlled and safe way, through play.

The real pirates of the mid-Atlantic *were* doing these unspeakable things - sexual perversion and criminal acts - and we can now see that they did them on behalf of the collective unconscious, for the society within which they existed was hugely repressed. That pirates were punished so brutally is testament to just how shameful those in power found it when their unconscious desires were acted out. That which they had tried to suppress came out in violent retribution against those who had made their darkness visible.

Wendy is also suffering from repression, but, as a child, it is one that has not yet ballooned into damaging neurosis. As the only woman in a group of 'savage' boys, it is clear that her position is hardly one of great freedom: this is pre-World War 1 London, where women still do not have the right to vote. Wendy's mother would have grown up in a world where she could not keep her own earnings, could not expect to graduate from university or enter a profession. Wendy's generation was literally then one of the first to begin to break through into greater equality - even though it would be another twenty years or more before they had equal voting rights to men. As she flies to Neverland, apparently away from this world of troubled womanhood that she is being forced to enter, she must have dreamt that she was escaping to a more equitable place. She then lands with a bump as it dawns on her that Peter Pan wants her to take on the female role and mother the lost boys - doing their laundry and providing comforts for them.

Neverland is thus not the escape from oppression that Wendy expects, although it is, for a short while, a TAZ space - a delicious bubble of freedom 'penetrated by the Marvellous,' as Bey puts it in his original essay. Wendy need no longer look longingly out of the window of her Kensington house, and no longer needs to be anxious about following her mother into a world where her finances and political opinions are all controlled by her father. She can fly freely, with this boy who has no shadow, and live a merry life - if only for a short while. Yet this wonderful sense of escape from the life that she fears entering is only short-lived: her role in Neverland becomes clear, and with the arrival of Hook, its status as a secure and safe place to live out her days is thrown into doubt. Death stalks the play: Wendy fears for her life at the hands of the pirates, and Pan's friend Tinkerbell is taken right to the edge of death - only to be resurrected by a surge in childhood belief in fairies. This isn't CS Lewis' *Narnia* either - time passes while their children are in Neverland, and Mr and Mrs Darling are left thinking that their children are dead, a fact that Wendy is acutely aware of, seeing their grief as she approaches the house again.

The lost boys and Wendy return to London and are welcomed in to the family, Wendy's mother seeing and recognising Pan as he leaves, reminding us that this journey from childhood into maturity is one that each generation must take. Barrie's pirates bring conflict and disorder into Neverland, but out of it comes a reinvigorated life. This is not about sexual and criminal eruptions, breaking through the far heavier economic and religious repression of the 18th Century. What we see in Barrie's play are, of course, more play-ful pirates, working to help young people navigate the difficult seas from childhood to adulthood. Yet pirates they are, and no matter how playful, their work remains that of unblocking Wendy's life at a pivotal time in her relationship with her father.

Removing the Mask

Why couldn't Wendy's parents lead her themselves? Why *did* her father insist they went out that fateful evening? It seems that he, in this small way, failed his daughter in her moment of need. Anxious about the move she needed to make, Wendy finds her parents absent - indulging their own desires at a dinner party, which her father needs to go to in order to further his career and secure the family economically - something he worries about greatly. The Wendy we meet is a girl who is disappointed by her parents. They have let her down, and there is understandable anger in her. They should have helped her on her journey, but instead they have abandoned her to look after her brothers while they worry themselves with money and social status.

And yet this is a narrative we find in countless stories: a child, parents absent, needing to undertake a significant journey. Why should this be the case? Part of the answer lies not in Neverland, but in 'a galaxy far far away,' where we find one Luke Skywalker dangling precariously from the underside of a large enemy space craft, his nemesis Darth Vader, towering above him, apparently about to strike him. Yet rather than cut him down with his light sabre, Vader reaches down a leathered glove to Luke:

Darth Vader: There is no escape. Don't make me destroy you. Luke, you do not yet realise your importance. You have only begun to discover your power. Join me, and I will complete your training. With our combined strength, we can end this destructive conflict and bring order to the galaxy.

Luke: I'll never join you.

Darth Vader: If you only knew the power of the Dark Side. Obi-Wan never told you what happened to your father.

Luke: He told me enough. He told me you killed him.

Darth Vader: No. I am your father.

Luke: No. No. It's not true. That's impossible.

Darth Vader: Search your feelings. You know it to be true.

Luke: Noooooooo!!!! Noooooooo!!!![3]

As with Wendy, we are spectators at a scene of parent-child turbulence. Whereas Wendy's disappointment at her parents' absence is more under the surface, here we see very clearly Luke - older than Wendy and more able to deal with more violent psychological themes - battling with a father who has let him down terribly. Yet this is not just disappointment in what his absent father has done, or failed to do. Nor is Luke's anguish here rooted in the horrible understanding that Vader is right, that he *is* Luke's father. The fear Luke has is the same that perhaps every son has: that becoming like his father is his unavoidable destiny.

Like Wendy, Luke is on the brink of maturity. For Wendy, this crucial moment was met with a parental retreat, whereas Luke has to face a parent intrusion. In the traditional way that Peter Pan is acted, Wendy's father turns into her nemesis; for Luke, just as he is about to push through into manhood, just as he has begun to discover his own power, his nemesis reveals himself as his father. Having Vader as his enemy was simple; now, as his father, he wants to take control of who Luke is to become, presenting him with an abysmal choice: become like Vader, or face destruction at his father's hands.

In psychological terms, Luke must confront the struggle to individuate from his father, whose dominating presence is like a black hole from which he is fighting to escape. Yet Vader's fears are on show here too. Luke's father wants to continue to live through his son, even if that means destroying his son's own dreams and passions for life in the process. His reasons for doing so are framed in terms of wanting to bring stability: 'we can end this destructive conflict and bring order...'

Just as every son fears becoming their father, so every father fears consuming their son to compensate for their own failures. As their sons grow up, they are confronted with their own finitude and struggle to find ways to leave longer lasting legacies: writing books, waging wars, building structures and forming inheritors. Whether this is Dawkins' 'Selfish Gene' or something else, Vader, like all fathers, aches for immortality, and sees in his son a way of preserving his own life, even if he is sickened by the price his son will have to pay: subsuming his own self in order for the father to carry on living through him.

Vader goes into battle with his son at a key moment. Luke has become a powerful figure and, by destroying the Death Star, has begun to flex his muscles in his rebellion against his father. He has thus proven himself to be a worthy inheritor, and yet, the father knows well, Luke is still lacking something. 'You have only begun to discover your power...I will complete your training' is thus the fulcrum that the father has been waiting for. His son is a worthy vessel who has begun to realise his own potency, and yet an incomplete one, and this presents the father with an opportunity to put himself forward as the 'patron' who will be able to complete him.

Vader thus comes to us as the very model of conservatism and orthodoxy. He wants to preserve the status quo, to bring order and consistency and to control the powers around him. It is perhaps unsurprising then that the writer, George Lucas (though he didn't actually direct or screen-write this film), chose to call the structure that Vader represents 'The Empire,' for it is in this empire politic that we see power being used to preserve the powerful, and conservative patronage being used to keep the economic and material situation stable for the already-wealthy from generation to generation.

Luke, for his part, has joined up with 'The Rebellion,' and it is within this Empire/Rebellion axis that we can begin to see Luke functioning within pirate archetype. Star Wars is full of piratic figures - Han Solo - notably rootless and fatherless - being one of them. Solo, for all the short and merry scrapes he has engaged in, is now 'dead' - frozen and given to the bounty hunter Bobba Fett to bargain with Jabba the Hutt. Luke, our other young pirate, is faced with the terrible decision about his future. His father, a powerful figure in the Empire, who want all trading in the galaxy to be controlled in their favour, wants him to come and join him, promising him stability and influence and a place in the aristocracy.

Yet, like all true pirates, Luke knows that to accept this offer would essentially mean his own death. While he might live, and escape the gallows, all that he stood for would be gone. He knows the decision he must take. He lets go. He falls. Vader, as far as we can tell, must assume that he is dead.

Yet Luke lives on. He is rescued by his sister, Princess Leia, and other rebels. However, this - and other parallel scenes in which Luke disappears, or is apparently mortally wounded, or frozen to death in a vast icy ocean - reinforces his pirate status. He has become the dead. His X-Wing ship perhaps a subtle nod to the crossed bones of the Jolly Roger, Luke now becomes far more fearful for Vader because he has stared death in the face, and taken its kiss. Wendy flew away and became as dead to her father, and Luke now does the same. He has refused to take his father's path, and so opened up the possibility that another path is possible.

As the film series draws to a close, Luke goes to battle against the Emperor himself. Seeing his son suffer, and perhaps impressed by the different road his actions have made conceivable, Vader's goodness is somehow restored: he kills the emperor, yet is himself mortally wounded. As he and Luke are reconciled, Vader asks Luke to remove the black mask. Luke does so, knowing that he is simultaneously killing the cyborg Vader - the dark side of his father - and, for a moment, revealing his true father, the flesh-only Anakin Skywalker again. By killing his father he is paradoxically restoring his father's humanity and Jedi integrity, a fact testified to at the close of the final film where we see Vader - Anakin Skywalker - taking his place among the other legendary Jedi warriors.

The power of Lucas' films lies in drawing together the roles pirates can play in challenging both economic and personal 'blockages.' The Empire wants to enclose all trade in the galaxy, removing people from the traditional lives they have known and making them subservient to the private enterprises of a small, powerful elite. At the same time, caught up in this, we have the story of an angry young man - Vader - who falls in with the Empire, and ends up in a struggle with his powerful young son who fundamentally disagrees with his principles.

Skywalker, a fictional farm-boy turned space pilot from a distant galaxy, is thus the best archetype we have so far for how pirates function, both in the material world and in the realm of personal development. Luke is not interested in overthrowing the Emperor in order to become a despot himself. As pirate, Luke lives by a higher code and is not after power for his own gain. What he is fighting for is the reinvigoration of the old order, a restoration of justice in a situation where violence and oppression has crept in. He does this working with the Rebellion, who fight from small, temporary outposts of freedom, scattered 'off the map' in the far corners of the Empire. His first major victory sees him courageously flying directly into the heart of the Death Star - laughing in the face of annihilation as he playfully fires his cannon, as if playing a game from his childhood. This is the piracy of economic unblocking and social liberty in all its glory.

Under the surface, however, Lucas develops a deeper narrative around the relationship between Luke and his father. Luke is not simply fighting to liberate tribes of people, or against an oppressive economic system. He is fighting his own father, the potent symbol of that system. In terms of personal development, for Luke to play pirate with his father means essentially to commit heresy against him. Luke rebels against his father's principles, against the values he lives by, and refuses to be subsumed into them. He rejects his father. He will not become like him.

And yet entwined in that rejection of Vader is a deeper desire Luke has to see his father redeemed. Although in his initial skirmishes he does want to kill him, as the series goes on we see that Luke spurns him *not* to destroy him, but to save him. The son's heresy brings the father's redemption. His rebellion against his father's empire brings about a renewed orthodoxy, and the family is restored. Darth Vader's mask and cloak gave him an aurora of power and superiority; Luke Skywalker's removal of these externals reduces Vader and returns him to his more humble place as Anakin Skywalker. He is given a human face once more.

Eye-Patches and Cardboard Cutlasses

What we see here in Wendy and Luke are the outlines of an established psychological process. As Jung explained, there can come a time in a child's development where they are beset by doubts and uncertainties. Their life can become 'blocked,' perhaps by parental failure, by disappointment in a 'big other.' In order to move into maturity the child must navigate this disappointment in some way. Violence is one option - Luke is tempted to kill his father in order to remove this 'blockage' - but both stories show a better way. The parent need not be killed; through the playful employment of pirates - who in their raw form are the very expression of a humanity unfettered and unrepressed - children can, without much trauma, redraw troublesome mothers and fathers with a more healthy perspective, diminishing them into something of an equal.

From the parents' side, this work by their children is hugely challenging. And yet all parents know, deep down, that this work must be done. And so, to begin it gently in them, we encourage our children to don their eye patches and arm themselves with cutlasses. All parents know that in order to grow up and make this journey from under their wings their children must commit heresy against them. Try as we might, we cannot do that work for them; because we are inevitably seen as part of the problem, we are the ones that they must vanquish.

All parents fail their children in some way, because all parents, all people, are imperfect. Indeed any therapist will tell you that having a *perfect* parent would in fact be *im*perfect for the child concerned, because they would not experience any lack or deficiency to draw them into maturity. Like the child kept away from any cough, cold or other virus, the 'perfect' parent ends up creating an aseptic child unable to cope with the realities of a very imperfect world outside the sterile cocoon they try to build around them.

And yet, ironically, it seems that this is precisely what parents have increasingly tried to achieve in the past 50 years, meaning that the move from adolescence to adulthood has become *more* difficult. Why has this happened? Contributing factors seem to be, ironically, the more shielded and coddled life that children now lead. Children have a reduced stage upon which they get to play. Fear about crime and abduction mean very few are able to play by themselves and create their own 'commons.' The locus of their playtime is now more virtual and commercial: shopping centres, game-worlds, television series. This is deemed 'safer' by those in power (though statistics reveal that this is barely the case and the perception that incidences of child abduction are on the rise is down to media influence) and this conveniently leads to greater income for them, with more televisions and computer games and devices sold. This has led to children becoming more static, less active, and less willing to take the sorts of risks that Wendy did, leaping out of a Kensington window for a life of adventure. Life is not as hard as it used to be, and while we welcome the safety and security that this brings, having removed all danger from their lives, young people are in danger of growing up unprepared for the adult world where they have to take these risks, and take responsibility for their own decisions and deal with the realities of failure, suffering and opposition.

In *The Quest for Human Meaning* Salvatore Maddi discusses how healthy development occurs when the impulses towards commitment, control and challenge are in balance. Being committed means feeling that 'by involving themselves actively in whatever is going on, [people] have the best chance of finding what is interesting and worthwhile to them.' Being in control means feeling that 'through struggle [people] can influence the outcomes of events going on around them.' Feeling challenged means believing that 'ultimately what is most fulfilling is to continue to grow in wisdom through what [people] learn from experiences, whether positive or negative.'[4] Ideally, parents need to develop each of these traits equally through their interactions with their children. In our busy world where work takes up so much of our time, and keeping abreast of digital connections so much of the rest, children are, literally, left to their own devices. In my experiences in schools, many children lack commitment, experience physical strength as the only method of control and shy away from challenge for fear of being seen as a failure. Another 'c' - 'consumption' is the most common substitute where these are lacking.

The practical outcome of this imbalance and immaturity in commitment, control and challenge is that children do not grow up well-equipped to cope well with the routine struggles of normal life. Traditionally, the early adult period is where very important, life-long decisions about marriage, career and lifestyle are made. In the realm of fairytales and the rich history of story-telling, the transition into maturity and marriage occurs after some struggle has been overcome. 'They lived happily ever after...' can only be penned once a battle has been won - whether that be over an evil step-mother, a scheming divinity or a hungry wolf. In the cotton-wool comfort of consumer-capitalist satiation, there is no struggle to overcome, perhaps except that of the over-bearing and neurotic modern parent. The removal of external difficulty, however well meant, leads to the extension of the infant stage. And yet, as this is accompanied simultaneously by the drawing back of the age of sexual exposure, children can face terrible confusion. They are in need of nothing, they are doted on and provided for, are safe and secure... and worshipped, and yet know in their guts - just as their parents do - that struggle and peril must be overcome if they are to truly grow up.

This is why they - with the full backing of their parents - are still drawn to pirates. Young people cannot look death in the face as the young conscripts in the trenches did, so pattern their skateboards with skulls and crossed bones, and smoke and listen to albums about gun crime and violence ironically flagged 'Parental Advisory.' Death has been frog-marched away by health and safety committees and careful safeguarding policies and soft landings in playgrounds... but is subconsciously waved back in the Jolly Rogers we find stitched into babygrows, in the cardboard cutlasses we arm our children with.

The ubiquitous popularity of pirates can be seen as an unconscious compensation for the over-safe world we have created. We provide our children with every last thing they could want, but then adorn these things with piratic images, leaving hidden signposts for them to understand that, though all struggle has been removed from their lives, they are going to need to engage in conflict as they grow up in order to work out who the hell they are. Wendy Darling and Luke Skywalker, girl and boy, are just two models we have from popular culture for this complex and difficult inner journey. Both of them fought battles with external foes, but the greater fight was their overcoming of the more personal monsters that their parents represented. In both cases, the pirate spirit was the disturbance that guided this battle in the right direction.

The key psychological question here is the focus of this battle. Given the disappointment and hurt all children are inevitably going to feel, to a greater or lesser extent about their parents, should they work to change their parents, or simply to move on themselves? Therapists are clear about this: if a child is going to focus their energies on seeking change in their parent - or any 'big other' - then they are going to experience persistent disappointment. What the child must do is move on from acting as a child and begin to function as an adult: making decisions and taking responsibility for themselves, regardless of what the parent may think. The hope is then that the parent will see the child behaving in this mature way, and the relationship will undergo healthy change - but as a secondary result. In terms of the example of Star Wars, what we see is Luke acting as this responsible, independent adult. Vader tries to 'patronise' him by insisting that he follows his way - but Luke makes his own decision and refuses to do as his father wishes. By not actually caring to change his father, by simply forging ahead with his own plan to destroy the Empire, he ends up, as a secondary effect, simultaneously challenging Vader to change, and opening a road whereby that change can happen. In a similar way, Wendy does nothing to try to change her father. She doesn't protest his going out, but rather flies away herself and, with Pan's help, overcomes the shadow of her father by defeating Hook.

Unblocking the Self

Just as pirates emerge when material systems become blocked, so they also appear - as cultural symbols or touchstones - when personal development becomes blocked too. The material and cultural commons are places in which rights are meant to be shared. When these begin to be enclosed for private gain people feel a sense of alienation and oppression, and the ground is ripe for piracy to flourish. In a parallel sense, the healthy Self is one in which the person feels free to give generously of themselves without any significant 'other' enclosing them and reducing their humanity. When a person feels depressed they are often feeling the weight of unfair or unrealistic expectation from a parent or person considered to be in authority over them, and they feel that their freedom to 'be' is reduced. Whether in transition from adolescence to adulthood, or from one relationship to another, a person can feel 'blocked,' and what the archetypal stories of Wendy and Luke show us is that, just as in the material realm, pirates can emerge here too to help fight for freedom.

However, it is important to understand the attitude that pirates have towards the systems that have oppressed them. Yes, Atlantic pirates attacked merchant vessels and naval ships that represented the economic and social structures that had been so brutal, but their flying of the Jolly Roger stated that this wasn't necessarily systematic retribution, a way of punishing the regime for their unjust actions. Rather it was to say 'we couldn't care less about you - we are dead to you, and you are dead to us.' Refusing to accept their lot as oppressed sailors, those who turned pirate were growing up and taking responsibility for their actions and lives. They knew and accepted the consequences, but refused to be cowed and patronised, refused to take the lowly position they were told was given them by God and refused to obey any longer the captains and officials who had ruled their lives so violently.

This is why, to return to Steve Jobs, he wanted to hire pirates. Pirates are able to copy, transform and combine precisely because of their relationship to death. Because they function as agents of decay they are able to break down dead material and prepare it for effective reuse. They are able to innovate and think laterally: they have the passion and drive to do something other than follow the line and come up with another product that is the obvious next iteration of the previous generation.

This was important for Jobs, looking to make Apple a company that thought differently from other technology businesses, but perhaps it was also important to him at a deeper level. Jobs was offered up for adoption by two young college students, who initially insisted that he be given to parents who themselves had had a college education. Finding out late on that the chosen adoptive parents were *not* graduates, his birth parents insisted that they promise to send him to college. This they did, but Jobs only lasted a term, deciding to drop out of any official degree programme and cut and paste different courses - including calligraphy and auditing - to suit his needs. He had already learned basic electronics, and how to work with his hands from his adoptive father, and his adopted mother - a pay clerk at a proto-Silicon Valley high tech firm - taught him to read before he had entered school. By the time he started Apple he had sifted through the various inheritances he had been given - a college-level brain, electronics, some business nous and a degree of self confidence - broken them down, rejected their dead orthodoxy (spending months in India in search of spiritual enlightenment, dropping acid and becoming a serious Zen Buddhist) and recycled their raw materials to create something brand new. He had, in other words, remixed his parents.

At both corporate and parental level, this is what Jobs was trying to achieve - though many would subsequently be highly critical of Apple for their patent battles and highly restrictive terms and conditions. (In another interesting pirate parallel, the designer and academic Nic Hughes has spoken of Apple's fixation with death. The governing aesthetic of Apple's products is that of the morgue: smooth, stainless steels and clinical whites, everything reduced down to the zero level.) Regardless of his success or otherwise, this piratic work of decay and reuse is, in both biological and psychological terms, what life and the rhythm of the generations is. Vader and others will try to freeze this, to stop it happening... but the pirate rebellion is the only true way of life continuing on and evolving.

Pirates were not trying to change the system, they were simply rejecting the lives they had been told they should live, and living the ones they thought they deserved. Rather than brutal, juvenile villains, pirates can be seen as bold and mature radicals who stood up and decided that enough was enough.

Similarly, in counselling rooms around the world, people are having to be guided through the difficult process of rejecting the lives that an over-bearing parent or significant other has demanded they lead, and stepping boldly into adulthood, into taking full responsibility for who they are and what decisions they take. Refusing to be primarily concerned with how this parent figure will react, they effectively 'leave them for dead.' Yet what they may or may not know is that it is precisely this act of psychological piracy that can lead to the redemption of this 'big other.' Maddi puts it this way:

> *'There are definite signs indicating when the psychotherapeutic process is complete. [...] The capstone is when the client assumes responsibility for their own lives, despite all the outside pressures that can easily be blamed for what happens to them, accepts that they are ultimately alone in their subjectivity, despite wonderfully stimulating efforts at intimacy, and faces that they will die, despite the heroism involved in creating meaning by choosing the future.'*[5]

Far from being a villain, the pirate, in Maddi's terms, is perhaps the most well balanced and mature person on the ship. Responsible, coping with pressure, intimate, heroic in forming the future, and open about their own finitude, Wendy and Luke both looked death in the face and overcame the blockages that their parents had left them. Leaving their parents for dead turned out to be the surest way to save them, and it was pirates who gave them courage to walk this path. And with our Jolly Roger t-shirts and pirate children's parties, we too are involved in this struggle to become the best we can be.

With consumer capitalism reaching ever further to enclose the material, cultural and relational commons our forebears took for granted, we need pirates more than ever to raise their swords and beat down the bankers and merchants who, with our tacit approval, have separated us from our own labour, and turned us from craftsmen and women into call-centre clones.

But, even with these fronts to fight on, there is one deeper and more ancient battle to wage to which pirates must be called again to our aid. It is a battle not with princes, nor captains, nor publishers, nor parents. It is the last and greatest battle of them all: the one with the gods themselves.

[*Pirate Baby Bottle, £8.99*]

6

Captain Odysseus

Playing Pirate with the Gods

The Way Back Home

It was a piratic raid that was to cost him dear. As he sailed to attack the Cicones on the island of Ismarus, to punish them for supporting his enemies in a recent war, the captain of a flotilla of Greek warships could not have known that doing so would see his journey home delayed by a whole decade. The war he had just finished - though some likened it to more of a series of pirate missions on strategic coastal communities - had itself been 10 years in the fighting, so this was some absence. But then again Odysseus, or Ulysses to the Romans, had raised the ire not just of Troy and its supporters, but of the community of gods looking on too.

Frustratingly for him, the bloody Trojan war had actually been started by these deities in the first place. Eris, the goddess of strife, had made a golden apple, a gift to be given to the goddess judged the fairest. Paris - a Trojan prince - had decided that Aphrodite should have it, because she promised to make Helen - the most beautiful woman on earth - fall in love with him. The problem was, Helen was already married, so when Paris took Helen to Troy, Agamemnon, king of Mycenae and Helen's brother in law, decided honour was at stake, so he set out to besiege Troy and get Helen back. Countless lives were lost, enormous suffering was caused, and many were displaced or traumatised. But, to add insult to injury, the gods who had started all this then cried out about the desecration of their temples in the battles that followed, and subjected men to their wrath.

Odysseus became a particular object of that anger. Though he had fought bravely in the war, a war which, though fought amongst men, was an attempt to restore what the gods had unbalanced, he fell from favour. Poseidon - a supporter of Troy - was angered by Odysseus' arrogance in victory and his subsequent sacking of the Cicones; Odysseus increased the divine wrath against him by killing Poseidon's son, the Cyclops Polyphemus. Thus his way back to Ithaca was blocked. Though he longed to return home and enjoy the simple pleasures of his land, his estate, his people, he was confined and confounded by divine powers.

His ships scuppered, his crew killed, Captain Odysseus endures his greatest and most difficult voyage, repeatedly coming up against gods who wanted to delay him, and women who wanted to seduce him. All the while, back home, a band of 108 suitors are trying to seduce his wife, Penelope, and pillaging his wealth through their constant gluttony. Though grieving as if he is dead, Penelope refuses their advances. Their son, Telemachus, is visited by Athena and given hope of his father's continued survival. He is instructed to get a ship together and go in search of him, and yet his journey eventually leads him back to Ithaca, and the old swine-herd Eumaeus, who is hiding Odysseus. Rejoicing and reunited, father and son return and slay the suitors. Odysseus is restored to Penelope, and peace returns to Ithaca.

Like many of the Greek myths the antiquity of *The Odyssey* narrative belies - or perhaps has informed - its psychological and spiritual maturity. Having explored some of the roots of the pirate archetype, we can now approach this complex pirate story equipped to consider some of its deeper meanings. Like the Vader-Skywalker and the Wendy-Mr Darling-Captain Hook stories, *The Odyssey* is about a father who is blocked, and who is again, surprisingly perhaps, led to release by his own child. Telemachus, in Greek, means 'far from battle' - and we can thus read into Odysseus' son an understanding that he is a slightly different person to his father. He is no pacifist, no. But his location in the story as distant from the goings on in Troy is significant as it places him apart from his father, with whom he wants to be reunited. Like Luke Skywalker, like Wendy, Telemachus leaves home on a quest involving an absent father. Yet he does so not out of some feud with the gods, but on the counsel of Athena.

Athena, like the rest of the cast of these myths, is not a straightforward character. However, her key traits tend to be that she dislikes fighting and prefers to use wisdom to settle disputes. She is the goddess of courage, civilisation, justice and just war, and also mathematics, craft and skill. She is, in other words, the antithesis of Poseidon - Odysseus' nemesis - who is the god of earthquakes and sea monsters, who loved war and was second only to Zeus in the number of illicit sexual liaisons he had.

Here is Odysseus' inner struggle set projected onto the canopy of heaven. On the one side is Poseidon, with his urges to war, power, destruction and sexual conquest, and on the other Athena, with her virtues of justice, wisdom and civilisation. With this in mind we might now consider, from a psychological perspective, what was *really* preventing Odysseus from returning to Ithaca. Although dressed up as a divine drama, with him as a pawn in their petty games, it was perhaps Odysseus' own struggles with himself that were blocking his own return.

Part of his saga begins at the point of his greatest hubris. Taunting the Cyclops Polyphemus, Poseidon's son, Odysseus tells him that his name is 'Nobody:'

> *"So, you ask me the name I'm known by, Cyclops?*
> *I will tell you. But you must give me a guest-gift*
> *as you've promised. Nobody - that's my name. Nobody -*
> *so my mother and father call me, all my friends." [...]*
> *They lumbered off, but laughter filled my heart*
> *to think how nobody's name - my great cunning stroke -*
> *had duped them one and all...*[1]

It is here, torturing and goading the son of a god, calling himself 'Nobody' as a joke to himself, because he really thought himself somebody, that Odysseus stokes Poseidon's ire. Remaining 'imprisoned' by various strong and alluring women, hiding his identity and only revealing it through a breakdown as he heard a poetic recital about the war he had long fought in, Odysseus can appear a man with a terribly blocked inner life, who would rather blame the gods for his inability to return home than take responsibility for his actions and struggles himself.

In his book *The Idolatry of God,* Peter Rollins explores how, in early child development, we experience a 'loss' or 'separation' when we come to realise that our mother's breast is not a physical part of us, that we are separate individuals. We grieve for this perceived sudden separation, yet in fact, there is no loss as we were never, in reality, anything other than separate.

> *'At this point, the world is experienced as "out there." With the advent of the "I," there is an experience of that which is "not I."*

So then the sense of selfhood is marked indelibly with the sense of separation. This means that one of our most basic and primal experiences of the world involves a sense of loss, for when we feel separated from something we assume that there was something we once had. The interesting thing to note, however, is that this sense of loss is actually an illusion, for we never actually lost anything. Why? Because there was no "me" before this experience of separation. Before the experience of loss there was no self to have enjoyed the union that we sense has been ripped away from us. The very birth of our subjectivity then signals a sense of losing something that we never had in the first place.'[2]

Rollins goes on to explain how this false loss creates in us a false urge to fill this false void. And religion - the creation of a system of divine other(s) who hold the strings to our lives - is one of the key ways that we do that. In the waters we have explored so far we have met pirates who did battle against the enclosure of the land that supported them and pirates who fought against the brutal exploitation of their labour in the Atlantic. We have also met pirates who fought to unshackle information from the powerful, liberate music from those who would try to own it and control access to it for profit and, in the previous chapter, pirates who spring from films and books to do inner work to release us from bonds that may have arisen through family or other relationships that hamper our personal development. Yet there are deeper centres of blockage and enclosure too, where the battle is not against an economic system or a media environment, nor even against the parts of ourselves that may have suffered through the way we have been brought up. The final battle is where we have to play pirate to the gods.

Some may feel that this is a skirmish which they have no need to join in, yet, even if people themselves carry no religious belief, it is very clear that we live in a world where religion and ideologies concerning a 'big other' still carry enormous importance. The militant Islamism of Al Qaeda, and the threat of terrorism that they still carry is a matter that should concern us, even if we are liberal atheists ourselves. Similarly, the move towards a highly conservative religious right in American politics is important the world over - just as is the evolution of Chinese communism as it explores the embrace of certain elements of capitalism.

These religions and ideologies are enormous and highly complex systems with long social and political histories. Yet, just as the battles pirates had with emerging globalisation boiled down to individual acts taken in individual levels, so our engagement against the enclosures that religions place on us must take place, first and foremost, at the personal level too. Capitalism gave birth to a separation between our labour and our rewards for that labour: what we did was no longer intimately tied in with a craft that we may have learned or with the substance of our humanity. We simply worked, and were paid. Yet a parallel process of separation took place deeper within us in our beliefs too. It is here, at the level of very personal separations, in the false voids we each have and each fill with false urges towards 'big others' whom we long to abdicate responsibility to, that we must allow pirates to work. So in reading *The Odyssey* we see that, having fought his big battles and played pirate with the Cicones, and, perhaps, the Trojans, Odysseus is now forced to face up to the profound blockage he has as a religious person. On the one hand he feels draw to war, to battles and beautiful women, yet he still feels the urge to go back to his wife in Ithaca and to the stable life of civil society. Unable to make a strong decision either way, his life becomes blocked and marooned: he moves from place to place, ostensibly trying to make it back home, but apparently stopped from doing so by various divine impediments.

In his own eyes Odysseus has become not just 'villain of all nations' but a villain of divinities too. The religious, meta-physical meta-narrative that he tells himself is that his return to comfort, to the theatre upon which he can to live out his days, to his commons, has been blocked by gods again and again. He is experiencing, to use Rollins' language, a profound separation and loss from some primal, original place - and has abdicated responsibility for what he is going through to some external, divine agency. And yet, when Telemachus *does* finally find him, he is *not* on some far-flung distant shore, but hiding away on Ithaca itself, with Eumaeus the swine-herd. His terrible separation is shown up to be not a separation at all. Why had he not simply gone home, to the very place he supposedly pined for? What had blocked him from these final few miles?

The tale that Homer tells is that Odysseus is afraid of the suitors who are pestering his wife and eating him out of house and home. Yet this excuse rings rather hollow. Odysseus is still the definitive man of the house, and husband to Penelope. He is a feared warrior and a highly respected citizen. Would the suitors really have the gall to challenge him? Any that did so would surely lose any chance of winning Penelope's heart.

Odysseus, wracked by a long war and the spiritual oppression of a religion that insisted he was fighting a divine cause, had become so enmeshed in the stories of these warring gods that he felt unable to overcome the separation he felt from his own home. Like Vader, Odysseus needed his son to play pirate with his beliefs. In practice this meant that Telemachus had to show his father that the separation he felt was really no separation at all, for he was *already* in Ithaca, he was already home.

We have already seen how the Atlantic pirates of the 18th century challenged the comfortable Christian practice of the ruling classes. They subverted their imagery in the creation of the Jolly Roger, and took such a radically different view of the value of life and the meaning of death that it petrified those in power, who responded by labelling them villains, to be rejected by the whole of humanity. And yet the irony was that their equitable treatment of men regardless of rank or class or disability, and their practice of wealth distribution, put them closer to the original message of the gospel than those who fawned in high churches, yet trampled on the poor.

Telemachus can be seen as performing a similar function. Though Homer's narrative presents him as still one who could be very violent, his name is significant in showing that he carried a different perspective on war, and on the gods too. Under the guidance of Athena, Telemachus is led to where Odysseus is hiding, although he doesn't yet recognise him. While Eumaeus is away, Athena restores something of Odysseus' youth to him, and tells him to present himself to Telemachus. He does so, and tells Telemachus everything that has happened. Then, Homer tells us,

> *'with those words Odysseus kissed his son*
> *And the tears streamed down his cheeks and wet the ground,*
> *Though before he'd always reined his emotions back.'*[3]

This is an important passage, because it reveals that Odysseus has changed. The transformation that Athena has worked to restore him to more youthful looks is significant, but perhaps only as a signifier of the inner work that has taken place. The warrior father, mentally scarred by so much violence, away from home and pulled one way then the other in his conflicting thoughts about power and masculinity, has these leathered and distressed coats stripped away, and a new, fresh surface revealed. This new Odysseus is now able to express his emotions, and not hold them back. Unfettered by the dead layers that had built up, he is finally able to confront the son he had been so absent from, and he breaks down in front of him.

We need to be clear here: this is a key turning point in the story, and represents a reinvigorated Odysseus who has broken free of some of the neuroses that bound him, but what follows is still a violent and complex tale. Father and son return home, Odysseus disguised as a poor beggar. The others mock him, and Penelope finally proposes a test: if any of them can string Odysseus' old bow, and shoot an arrow through twelve axes, she will accept them. Odysseus is the only one who can, and he turns the bow on the suitors, who are then all killed. It is gory stuff, and references to the gods are peppered throughout, yet there are differences here too. Odysseus is no longer the passive victim, trapped and taunted by the gods. His return home as a beggar is a mirror of his arrogant joke to Polyphemus that he was 'Nobody.' Now he *is* nobody, but can, from that humble position, begin to become again who he really is meant to be.

The Odyssey reveals to us something of a litmus test for works of genuine piracy: the old order ends up transformed and reinvigorated. Yet there is a deeper archetype to uncover here too. Looking at the story from a psychological angle, we note that it is the heresy of the child that brings the parent's redemption, and this pattern is repeated in the *Star Wars* films and *Peter Pan* too. In the case of the Skywalker family, we see Darth Vader-Anakin Skywalker's redemption and release from the enclosing black mask at the end of the series of films. With the Darlings we see Wendy return home and move towards her mother, who in her own blocked youth had met Pan. These are the happy endings, satisfying conclusions where, just as Telemachus and Odysseus together bring renewal to their home, the listener is left in no doubt that the world within which the story has occurred is now a better place than it was at its frustrated beginning, and this regeneration, this unblocking of something that was preventing the family or grouping to move on, is precipitated *not* by some courageous act of the parent, but by an act by the child which is experienced as heresy. For example, when Telemachus arrives at Eumaeus' house, he refuses to take Odysseus' seat, and is generous to a fault – promising, despite the suitors ravaging his house, to clothe and feed him and set him on his way. Odysseus' heart is 'by god, torn to pieces' hearing this. (Book 16, line 103) There is regeneration here, and a dismantling of the religious narratives that had bound Odysseus, yet, after all his travels and travails, it ends with his son providing the key to finally unlock his heart and allow him to truly come home. That home, we might suggest from reflection on Salvatore Maddi's work on *The Quest for Human Meaning* in the previous chapter, is a place where the three dimensions of commitment, control and challenge are all in balance - in high contrast to the warring, rootless 'quest' Odysseus has experienced, where all of these elements were distorted, and these distortions were sanctified by the gods.

The Tragedy of the Prodigal Son

Odysseus, we are led to believe at the end of Homer's epic, does find peace at last. Yet these stories of playing pirate with a blocked life do not always end happily. There will surely be parables or religious legends from many faiths that could be mustered as examples here. My own experience, and thus my own journey of piratic engagement, is within the Christian tradition, where we find a parallel story to that of the journey-and-return narrative of *The Odyssey* in the story Jesus told of the prodigal son. The traditional telling frames it as one of gracious restoration, as brilliantly and loving expounded by Henri Nouwen in his extended meditation on Rembrant's painting, *The Return of the Prodigal Son*. The basic plot may be familiar: a young man commits a terrible act of heresy against his doting father. He approaches him to ask for an early payment of his inheritance - an act that, in true pirate style, signifies that his father has already become dead to him. The father consents, and the son goes off, squanders the money in wild living before falling on hard times, whereupon he decides to return home. His father has been watching out for him and, even though his oldest son is scornful and resentful, the father welcomes the young son back into the family, throws a huge feast, and declares that 'this brother of yours was dead, and is alive again; he was lost and is found.'[4]

Nouwen's 'light' reading of this parable is that it is really about the journey that both sons must make towards becoming fathers themselves. It is a journey from youth to parenthood, from wild living on the younger son's side, and resentful labour on the older son's side, to gracious, generous, forgiving love that the father models.

However, I believe that, reading Luke's words in parallel with *The Odyssey* - and Luke, as a man well educated in Greek culture, must have been familiar with it - we can uncover a 'dark' inverted version of this parable, which presents the son's journey from youth to adulthood not as one of heresy and redemption, but as a tragedy, as a failed act of piracy and an unsuccessful attempt to escape from and change the powerful draw of his father's empire.

Luke begins his story 'there was a man...' and we can thus see the perspective from which the story is being told. Luke could have had Jesus beginning 'there was a young man...' but he chooses not to. We should perhaps not read too much into this, other than to mention the adage that most history is written from the point of view of the powerful, and we might hint that the 'light' version of the parable, the reading where the son is lost and resurrected, is very much the father's reading. He is overjoyed, has compassion for his son, and celebrates his return to the family empire with a large and lavish feast.

Our 'dark' reading is an attempt to see the same events from the point of view of the young son. He had a grouchy and overly-dutiful older brother who had no choice, as the first-born, *but* to work in the family business. But our younger son had a bigger vision. He knew that there was a wider world outside of the safe and comfortable empire that his father had built. So he approached him, and asked for his inheritance. This, he knew, would be like a dagger to his father's heart. The property his father had built up would have to be split prematurely, potentially forcing his father and older brother to live more modestly. There is no great detail given about the true state of the father's estate, but we do know that the end of the story sees the son returning to a situation where there were hired servants, a fattened calf, music and worked land. In other words, the young son, awful as his request was, most likely knew that the estate that would remain after the split was still large enough to sustain some level of wealth.

The story also carries no mention of what the son's intentions might have been when he asks for his inheritance. It was some time after he had received his share that he 'got together all he had...' It is not impossible that the father viewed his son's request as him taking some initiative and being something of an entrepreneur. The boy might even achieve a good return, and add to the family's riches. The next parable Luke places in his gospel narrative is that of the 'shrewd manager,' who was profoundly dishonest and underhand in his dealings with his master's finances, and yet was commended for it. Jesus' concluding remarks on the story are quite shocking: 'I tell you, use worldly wealth to gain friends for yourselves, so that when it is gone, you will be welcomed into eternal dwellings.'[5]

The economics in these parables are not straightforward, and certainly do not always carry convenient moral platitudes. So, while the 'light' reading of the prodigal story is able to carry the message of the father's generosity, the context within which it is placed does allow the 'dark' reading to sustain a more complex economic narrative. Perhaps, we might imagine, taking the young son as protagonist, he had hated the wealth that his father had pooled for himself, and had always dreamed of sharing it more widely. He had lived all his life in the comfortable, walled compound that his father had built - an empire he claimed he had created through efficient land management and astute economies of scale - but perhaps the son saw the injustice here, and thought it amounted to sweat-shop labour and class discipline. We can imagine him looking at his own future: his father and older brother worked so hard there was a deadness in their eyes... he didn't want to die that way. He had to get out. He asked for his share of the property (though whether that meant actual land assets is unclear) and his father agreed. Once things had settled, he liquidated the lot, and left, for the first time feeling truly free. He celebrated in style by spending wildly and generously, sharing out the money that had lain gathering cobwebs, letting it all go with an extravagant potlatch. He took Jesus' words to heart: used his worldly wealth to find friends... Far better than keeping it locked away, isolated and cold.

Building on this different perspective on the son's motivations, we might wonder if he wanted to do useful work where it was really needed. Like an ancient Christopher McCandless, here was an idealist wanting to step out from his privileged background, explore a wider world and do something more authentic. If he hadn't sought out a more 'real' life, it certainly soon found him. Famine struck. The friends he had bought disappeared and he was left with nothing. This was hardship like he had never known, but resisting the urge to go back to the dead comfort under his father's wing, he hired himself out and got on with honest labour. It was shitty work, with the very animals his father had always despised, and he was constantly hungry. He'd never known hunger before, and even sat for a while in the animal feeder, considered eating the pods that the pigs had to fatten them up for some wealthy bastard who still ate well.

It was too much, too soon. In an area of famine no one had anything they could share with him, and nor did he deserve it more than they. So rather than be an extra burden, he came up with a compromise: he would never live freely off his father's riches again, but he could return as a servant. This way he could rebuild his strength, and do so with honest labour. More than that, he could show his father the error of his father's ways, tell him about the hungry people that lay dying not so far away, and turn his father's heart to compassion for them.

So the son returned home. But his father saw him coming. He'd watched every day, worried about the ideas he might come back with, concerned that his other son's head might also be turned. All he had worked for and gathered around himself was at stake. He could not risk it being redistributed in some ridiculous lefty scheme.

As it happened, he needn't have worried. The young son was tired, thirsty and splintered. He could only speak with half a heart, and the ideas that had felt so clear and sharp far from home now felt confused and tumid. His father refused his pleas to have him work. He gave him a warm robe, which, if a little heavy on his thinned frame, felt sumptuously comfortable. He was given the family signet ring, which invested him with an odd feeling of pride. He was someone again, with a strange but alluring sense of power. There didn't seem to be the time or place to challenge his father and persuade him to widen the radius of his generosity...and so he settled back into his old ways, and accepted his old seat at the large and loaded dinner table.

'*I was alive*,' the young man said to himself as he sat listening to his father toasting his return at the feast... '*but now I am dead again*.' His older brother seemed disappointed and angry, and his head hung low as the music raged and his father grew enraged. He'd tried to break out and had failed; he'd let both of them down. His plan to escape was in tatters. It was over. The father was too strong. They would both become like him.

This is another story about children and parents, but, unlike *Peter Pan* or *Star Wars*, here is an attempt to play pirate that ends in tragedy, for the old order defeats the rebellion of the young son and, as the story closes, the empire is sustained. We should take careful note here: not all pirates should be valorised, for not all piracy ends with regeneration of the commons nor lives reinvigorated. Some, like the prodigal son, launch out as pirates, but then find the cost too high, and soon take refuge in the economics of the old order they set out to critique. The prodigal's life - and he is a prodigy perhaps, one with prodigious vision and talent - is presented in the opening of the tale as blocked by the father. Only his symbolic killing permits the son to break free. He *almost* escapes the father's gravity, but the draw of power and comfort is too much. Rather than being a redemptive story of a lost son who returns to his senses, in our dark reading, this parable can be explored as a tragedy about a young pirate who left the legal strangulation of father's deadening empire, *did* experience sensation for a while, lived a 'short but merry life' and yet eventually fell back into the temptation of the trappings of wealth... via a stint in the service of a swineherd.

Whether Luke meant it or not, the tale he wrote has fascinating parallels with *The Odyssey*. In both stories we have a father and son who are 'blocked' - although, again in both stories, it is only really the son who appreciates properly the truly nature of that blockage. In both stories we have one party who has departed, and thus created some dramatic separation and tension between the two protagonists. But this is where the stories differ, for only in *The Odyssey* does one step out and go in search of the other. In the prodigal son, the father watches out for his son's return, but never appears to leave the boundaries of his property to find him. This is odd, because the preceding two parables in Luke's gospel give us a shepherd who leaves the flock of 99 to go on an exhaustive search for the single sheep who has strayed, and a women searching for a prized lost coin, who empties her whole house on to the street in order to find it. Yet in the parable of the prodigal son the father remains rather passive.

Telemachus, on the other hand, goes on a journey to find his father - an act of compassion and active empathy that is missing in the prodigal son, whose attempts to play pirate with his father's empire appear born of more selfish things. Both stories, oddly, appear to turn on decisions made while in a degrading place: working with pigs. Pirates have always been born in places of oppression and dirt, and it is here, in amongst the filth and the grunting, that true character is shown. For Odysseus and Telemachus, there is a decision to change. Odysseus sees that he must go home - indeed, that he *can* go home. The separation he thought he knew from Ithaca was an illusion. His blocked life is released. The young prodigal, however, sitting among the pig feed, decides on compromise. 'I am no longer worthy to be called your son, make me like one of your hired men.' He won't change his father; his father has changed him.

Pirates among Pirates

What is it that enables change in one story, and not the other? One possibility is the difference between the place of women in the two stories. In Luke's prodigal story, all mention of women has been expunged. Other than hints we might take of them involved in the son's 'wild living,' and the older son's accusations of his brother using prostitutes, there are no female characters at all. This is in contrast to *The Odyssey*, where Odysseus' wife Penelope is the calm fulcrum around which the whole tale balances, and Athena is the goddess (of philosophy and just war) whose interventions are the key to the unlocking of the narrative.

It is here that it is right to digress a moment and discuss why it might be that so few women are mentioned in traditional pirate literature. History, as we have already noted, is written from the point of view of the powerful and, as far as the empire-builders of England and Spain were concerned, women had no significant role to play. They could not vote and women of any social position were never expected to work or do anything of much interest whatsoever. They were reduced to sexual objects. The Trojan war was fought over a beauty contest, and women were not allowed on naval vessels lest they caused lustful argument. Yet, in the end, it is Athena who brings peace, careful thought and justice; it is Wendy's mother - and Wendy - who meet Peter Pan and make the moves to unblock their family, and it is Luke Skywalker's sister, Princess Leia, who is the calm, intelligent diplomat.

Women struggled in these worlds - and still do - because the force of male power was so strong. But many, like Anne Bonny and Mary Read, did break through, becoming pirates among pirates - unblocking the enclosed the life that others had set out for them and living lives of adventure and drama.

Almost all the information we have about Anne Bonny is based on Captain Johnson's *General History*, so verifiable facts are difficult to come by. Johnson has her born in Ireland and then moving to North America where her mother died. Her father initially struggled, but then made a substantial fortune as a merchant and Anne was considered a very eligible young woman. However, she ran off with a young and poor pirate, James Bonny, and ended up in the Bahamas - a sanctuary for English pirates. At some point around 1718 she started a relationship with the pirate John Rackham, and with Mary Read the three of them stole the *Revenge* and began gathering a crew.

Mary Read had had a less fortunate upbringing. Born 'illegitimately' to the widow of a sea captain. Her older brother - of more acceptable birth - then died, so, to keep inheritance payments coming in from his grandfather, Mary's mother pretended that Mary was the son, and dressed her as a boy. She remained cross-dressed while she worked as a footman, and later a sailor. Joining the British army, she fought bravely and then fell in love with a Flemish soldier - dressing as a woman for the first time when they were married. He unfortunately died, so Mary returned to male dress and took passage on a ship to the West Indies. They were intercepted by pirates - Rackham and Bonny - and Mary was forced to join them. It was only after Bonny became very keen on her that Read told her she was a woman. To prevent Rackham becoming jealous, he too was let in on the secret.

As women and pirates life was doubly tough for Bonny and Read. Pirates were hated with a passion, and women who took on men's work equally so. Yet it can be argued that their legacy is a significant one. Their lives were documented by Captain Johnson, and the Dutch and French editions of his *Historie der Engelsche Zee-Roovers* carried an engraving of Bonny, showing a bare-breasted female pirate carrying a sword and torch, pushing forwards beneath a Jolly Roger, some official royal decree being trampled under her foot. On one side of her are fellow pirates, hung on gallows, and on the other a burning ship. The direct link is impossible to make, but it seems likely that this scene was the inspiration for Eugéne Delacroix's famous painting of the French Revolution *Liberté Guidant Le Peuple* - Liberty Leading The People - which came to symbolise one of the great uprisings against oppressive empirical power in modern history.

Marcus Rediker writes:

'It seems that the liberty seized by Anne Bonny and Mary Read - the liberty they found so briefly, so tantalisingly, beneath the Jolly Roger - took a strange, crooked path from the rough rolling

deck of a ship in the Caribbean to the polished, steady floor of an art salon in Paris.'[6]

Women were often denigrated as no more than pretty objects or child-makers by those in power, yet the power of these two connected pictures shows them as central to the rhythm of life and socio-political renewal. Marching under the Jolly Roger in the engraving, marching under the Tricolore in the painting, brave women are seen as leading people onward through traumatic change, through death and social upheaval. This is not the violent revolution of the masculine soldier, but the determined re-naissance of the feminine mutineer. Their ability to give birth is matched with their courage to provide the necessary link between death that surrounds them in fallen fighters and hung pirates, and new life. It is women who allow the rhythm of renewal to continue.

To return to the parable of the prodigal son, the lack of women in the story means that the motifs of death - the father becoming dead to the son as the son asks for his inheritance, and the son dying again as he returns to the feasting table - are given no balance by feminine characters, meaning that no new life is possible. The story is sterile; the sons and their father are stuck. In contrast, though Odysseus is a brave warrior, he is utterly unable to find release from his situation without the intervention of Athena. Similarly, Telemachus - though similarly brave - is unable to leave Ithaca to find his father without her encouragement. All the while Penelope remains constant and faithful as the suitors harangue her and demand she give up on her husband and child.

Though their names are often passed over, it is these radicals - the historical Anne Bonny and Mary Read and the fictional Princess Leia and Athena - who carry the vital link between one generation and the next, and thus create the conditions within which the rhythm of death and rebirth is made possible. It is only with their feminine influence that narratives can be balanced, so that the heresy of the child can bring the parent's redemption, and thus the cycle of life continue towards greater maturity.

The Divine Pirate

It is thus the women who make the difference between the triumph of *The Odyssey* and the tragedy of the prodigal son, and it is perhaps this lack of femininity in the way that the Christian West developed that has led to such continued blockages and enclosures.

This is a church that is only just beginning to accept women as leaders, a church that has historically made women remain silent and covered up. And yet central to the crucifixion and resurrection narrative is a woman who resolutely does not remain silent, and - in traditional tellings - certainly had not always remained covered up. Mary Magdalene had had 'seven demons' cast out from her, though there is no evidence to support her status as a prostitute - something that appears to have been invented in the 6th century. Regardless, it was her who was the first witness to Jesus' resurrection - a 'rebellious' woman who again stands at the interface between death and new life.

Given this central place of one Mary at the nativity and another at the resurrection, it seems extraordinary that Christianity for so long rejected women in leadership and repressed their contributions to the growth of the faith. By doing so, however, we can now see that it is no surprise that much of Christianity has been a force for conservatism. With a Christian theology that sees the return of the prodigal son as a good thing, we see a tradition which venerates the masculine conservation of the empire, rather than a more feminine rhythm of heresy-fuelled renewal.

A good example of this can be seen in the male-dominated priesthood of the Church of England. Begun as a Protestant schism from the Catholic Church in 1534, arguments continued between those in seats of power as to the extent of its Reformed or Catholic leanings. By the time its Thirty Nine Articles had been published in 1563, its doctrine had settled down, and England became more consistently Protestant.

As the sociologist and economist Max Weber saw it, this move to Protestantism was an important factor in the adoption of capitalism – and thus the expansion of empire. The old Catholic theology of salvation assured people of their place in heaven if they simply received the sacraments and obeyed religious authority. With Calvin and Luther sweeping those assurances away, people needed other means of becoming confident in their salvation, and hard work at one's 'vocation' or 'calling' became the main ways in which people gained this. With economic success being a sign of successful and fruitful labour, the Protestant work ethic paved the way for modern modes of organised labour and the capitalist systems of waged work.

Equally importantly, Martin Luther emphasised the individual nature of salvation, and coupled with the impact that Protestant beliefs had on economics, the sense of shared labour on a 'commons' was replaced by individual graft for personal gain. Indeed, the new Protestant Church of England seemed so intertwined with capitalism and the enclosure of property, that the penultimate statement in its Thirty Nine articles - its list of core doctrines - makes it absolutely clear that it is 'anti-commons':

> *The Riches and Goods of Christians are not common, as touching the right, title, and possession of the same as certain Anabaptists do falsely boast.*

What I have worked hard for, to assure myself and others of my worth for salvation, is mine and mine alone.

What is remarkable is just how completely at odds this is with the practice of the early church, where we read that 'all the believers were together and had everything in common. Selling their possessions and goods, they gave to anyone as they had need.' [Acts 2:44, 45]

It is possible to see hints here of the same struggle that the prodigal son engaged with – and similarly failed to conquer. The young son, like the young church, can be seen to have attempted a radical departure from the socio-economic and religious structures that enclosed them. Branded as heretics who risked pulling the house down on everyone, their practices were denigrated as filthy and disgusting by those who considered themselves morally superior.

The early church was ridiculed and despised and rumours abounded that they ate flesh and drank blood, and that they were morally deviant. Their 'parent' – the orthodox Judaism of the day – was a religion which Jesus himself had pronounced 'blocked.' Pharisees and Sadducees were denounced as little more than 'white-washed sepulchres' – images of undecaying death again – and criticised for loading common people with intricate and complex laws, while not following these laws themselves. The temple in Jerusalem was also attacked for its injustices. The gospels relate an episode where Jesus got so angry that he turned over the tables of the money-changers in the temple forecourts, and drove out the religious peddlers with a whip. As I have argued in a previous book *The Complex Christ*, this should not be seen as a 'cleansing' *of* the temple, but rather as Jesus unblocking the way *into* the cleansing that the temple was meant to offer. Here was religious capitalism at its worst: worshippers had to buy 'clean' temple money at unfair rates, in order to purchase specially purified (and thus expensive) animals which could then be sacrificed. It was a money-making scam, an enclosure of temple practice for profit.

The early church can therefore be seen in pirate terms as a community of men and women who went 'on the account.' They declared mutiny against the religious powers that had enclosed them, and, using the teachings of their leader, departed from Jewish orthodoxy into the heretical waters of an inclusive Christianity based on 'the commons.' Just as the Atlantic pirates were hunted down and executed in gruesome ways as a warning to others not to join their revolt, so the early Christians were rounded up and publicly stoned to death too – just as their leader had been. Crucifixion was the gallows of the day – public, horrific and often slow. Jesus was taken to Golgotha - 'the place of the skull' - and with two bandits three beams were raised like masts against the sky. With the crossed bones of the condemned this was the Jolly Roger acted out in all its gore. Jesus was crucified for the simple reason that his teachings threatened the power of the Jewish religious leaders. He declared that people could be forgiven without having to spend money on expensive sacrifices. He challenged the Jewish classifications of what was 'clean' and 'dirty' – and thus what was acceptable and unacceptable. These heresies were not only objectionable to the religious beliefs of the Pharisees and other leaders, they also threatened their power to control believers, and thus their status and wealth too. Like the English monarchs of the early 18th Century, those who diverted income streams away from the empire and inspired lowly labourers to consider themselves free, needed to be got rid of, and done so in ways that would deter others from following them.

It is likely that the deterrent was effective to some extent. The first Christians were full of fear in the days immediately after the crucifixion, and scattered. They found strength and verve later, but, as with the prodigal son, power and personal comforts were finally the undoing of radical, early Christianity. Having been opposed by Jerusalem, and then by Rome, Christianity eventually became the religion of empire, and quickly settled into the easy throne of fattened calves, of comfortable robes and jewellery. The tragedy of the prodigal son is thus the tragedy of the church: a radical departure that resolved, through an act of heresy, to bring renewal to a deadened Judaism, yet quickly lost heart and returned to the temptations of power and comfort.

This was not how it was meant to be.

Returning again to the pivotal parallel moment with Odysseus hiding out with the swineherd, and the prodigal son lying filthy among the livestock, it is hard not to assume that Jesus may have been alluding in his parable to his own beginnings, born into a stable. In his telling of the tale, Jesus surely recognised himself in the young son.

Taking a traditional Trinitarian view for a moment, as the familiar nativity story tells it, Jesus had walked away from heaven, from his own Ithaca, from his own paradise, and landed, naked, poor and hungry in a manger, totally dependent on the generosity of others. He came to earth from a place of comfort and experienced hunger, saw suffering, and knew pain. He came from a 'kingdom of heaven' into an occupied territory, where he was excluded, disenfranchised, and, in all likelihood, economically exploited. Yet, born as a Jew, he also entered a religion that had a long history of divine violence, of exile and bloody wars and power abuse and petty arguments about doctrine, as well as bigotry, racism and sexism. As son of the 'Father God' whom Jews worshipped, he knew that all of this had been to his benefit. Yet the few vignettes we have, looking in on Jesus growing up, we see someone changing their thinking on what this temple religion meant.

The first time we see Jesus entering a temple or synagogue is when, as an adolescent, he leaves his parents to spend time with the teachers of the Law. 'Didn't you know I had to be in my Father's house?' was his reply when Mary and Joseph asked where he had been. Here was a faithful young boy - keen to learn from wise elders and clearly considering the temple - the centre of worship of his Father - as his true home.

Later we see him in a local synagogue at the beginning of his ministry, reading from the prophet Isaiah:

> *'The Spirit of the Lord is on me, because he has anointed me to preach good news to the poor. He has sent me to proclaim freedom for the prisoners and recovery of sight for the blind, to release the oppressed...'* [Luke 4: 18]

This is a classic pirate text, full of unblocking and the breaking of oppressive practices. The interpretation that he placed on it - personalising the text, and claiming it fulfilled by himself - outraged those who heard it, and he was driven out of his home town as a result. Here is someone who is clearly radicalised and not the loyal, supplicant believer any longer. His message is not centred around time spent in dedicated worship and contemplation in the temple, but about social justice and release from captivity.

Jesus gradually grew up to experience Judaism - the religion that worshipped his father as God - as blocked and oppressive. It kept the poor in their place, and the powerful in theirs. What would he do? As he prayed in the wilderness, and subsequently in the Garden of Gethsemane, he knew he had a decision to make. Hungry, tired and alone, here was his temptation: to return to his father having changed nothing. He could accept his father's mantle with the old order still intact, and thus accept power and influence and the trappings of both. He could do that... or he could commit heresy against that old order, and reveal it for what it was: a form of social control which served to keep a priestly elite well fed and very wealthy, while loading the poor with endless rules about what they could and could not do - and how to pay for forgiveness if they did err.

In the final vignette we see Jesus approaching the temple in Jerusalem, disgusted, as we have seen, at the exploitative economics at work at the money-changers tables. This is Jesus returning to the place he had visited as a child and 'beating the bounds' - smashing down enclosures and barriers that kept the poor from their common place of worship. This, we must remember, was the place the young Jesus had considered to be his home. And now he was returning to break down its high walls to allow free access to the riches within, riches that had been blocked and enclosed by those who guarded the gates.

Unmasking the Father

Jesus' passion can be read as the story of paternal piratic action *par excellence*, for Jesus *does* refuse to compromise, *does* commit terrible heresy against the empire's enforcers - simultaneously refusing to play along with the Empire of Roman rule, and sacking the money-changing tables in the temple in true buccaneer style. It was very likely this act of protest in the temple courts that led to his arrest and crucifixion. In taking a whip to the money-changers who worked in the courts of his Father's house we see Jesus' dramatic decision to not give in to the temptation to let the religious status quo remain. It is here that we see him acting differently to the prodigal son, and thus avoiding the tragedy of another young man failing to overcome the draw of power and comfort offered by the distortion of his father's empire. No. He would follow through with his piratic act, and live as if everything the temple stood for was dead, was fallen.

Jesus embraces death; the place of crucifixion standing like mast and cross-beam from which a skull and crossed-bones hung. After a 'short but merry life', penetrated by the marvellous, he is crucified by the Romans and Jews as a heretic. St Paul writes that Jesus 'became sin' - like Odysseus he is the villain not just of all nations, but of God too. Yet, as we know from the pirate archetype, his actions will bring renewal to that dead orthodoxy. By beating the bounds of the temple, by subverting those who hoped to enclose religious practice for their own benefit, Jesus aimed to open up the commons of heaven again. (Yet, as we can now see, it can only do that through the courage of brave and faithful women: the Mary who gave birth to him, and the Mary who was the first to announce his resurrection.)

The philosopher Slavoj Žižek has written of how this heretical work of Jesus as God's son allows God 'to see himself through the distorting human perspective.'[7] In other words, the traditional idea of the incarnation being as if God brought a piece of heaven down to purify the earth is reversed: Jesus' tortured body rips open the easy paradise of heaven to allow a little earthly dirt to enter and do its work of reinvigoration. This is the incarnation as a truly piratic act. Through his miracles and highly controversial teachings Jesus subverts the blocked orthodoxy of his father's empire through a series of happenings - TAZs if you will - that are totally outside 'the law' as it stood, yet are about the restoration of freedom to those who have been oppressed. This true kernel of Christianity has been almost entirely lost, and it has become a religion just as blocked as any other, yet its roots place it not within a western capitalism that seeks to pool resources for the few, but within a revolutionary society that looks to return the commons to the people.

We have already seen how Telemachus' act of piracy - his 'distance from battle' and setting sail under the banner of careful thought - exposed Odysseus' separation as a myth. He was already home in Ithaca and had simply to admit that to himself and live as such. With reference to Peter Rollins' writing, we have already explored this myth of separation within each of us, and how religions rise to attempt to fill that gap we perceive between us and the gods. However, Rollins goes even further and proposes a radical extension.

The sense of loss between ourself and our mother is itself a loss that has to be lost, because the separation between us was never anything else. In a similar way, on the theological plane, Jesus' death is not to be seen as some kind of sacrifice that crosses the gap between us and the divine, but an event that explodes the myth that there was even a separation to grieve between us and God in the first place.

There is a dramatic visual expression of this at the moment of Jesus' death. As he breathes his last, the curtain in the Jewish temple ripped from top to bottom. This curtain separated off 'the holy of holies' - the very place where God's presence was said by the Jews to dwell - so this tearing open of that material expression of separation was a radical enactment of the destruction of the barrier between humanity and God. Traditionally, the ripping of the curtain has been taken to symbolise how, through Jesus' death, God was able to 'escape' this enclosed space and begin to dwell amongst his people without the need for priests or religious structures. But there is a more radical interpretation: the rent curtain can be seen as Jesus 'unmasking' his father God and exposing the reality behind the screen. In this reading, it is not that God was there and escaped; rather, the pulling back of this veil that separated common humanity from the 'holy of holies' exposed as false the myth that God had even been there behind the curtain all along.

In rather beautiful symmetry this potent image of ripped fabric carried through into the radical actions of protesting sailors. Inspired by pirate rebellions, sailors on merchant vessels refused to be brutalised any longer and, in protest against the powers and structures that had done so much violence against them, ripped the sails of their ships from top to bottom. This 'striking' of the sails, from which the idea of a strike as industrial dispute comes, was an exposure of the essential emptiness of the merchants' threats. The ripped fabric billowed freely and the ship would not move. For all their pomp and power, the merchants and princes were nothing without the labour of working men, and the striking of the sails was a powerful symbol of the puncturing of the pretence that it was ever otherwise.

In a similar way, with the ripping of the temple curtain, the 'bogey man' God that the High Priests had espoused was punctured and deflated. They had preached a religion of an angry God who needed placating with sacrifices, and was so intolerant that only the most holy, perfect priest could enter this special place once a year. This amounted to enormous social control: the priests could demand certain behaviours of the people, and levy taxes and other 'offerings' from them too in return for promises of forgiveness.

Jesus' willingness to face up to every threat and scare tactic that this empire can throw at him – eventually leading to him being handed over and killed - leads to the ripping open of that empire's desolate heart. And yet, even as they do their worst and kill him, the threatened apocalypse does not come. The curtain is torn, the light pours in and the Emperor's inner sanctum is exposed as empty. Just as we see at the end of the story of *The Wizard of Oz*, there *was* no emperor after all, just a system by which his myth allowed those in power to remain so.

We have seen how the Jolly Roger was a standard raised that announced that those who sailed under it embraced the Empire and powers of this world as dead. Now, in this pirated view of Jesus' cross, we can see it as a standard raised that those who live by it embrace the death of religion too. The crucifixion explodes the myth of an angry, hidden, divine other. God is unmasked, yet this is no cause for grief.

Odysseus was free to go home, because the gods that he thought were binding him were no more than the ties he himself had made. And for those first Christians, this revelation of the death of religion brought an extraordinary new way of being that was no longer bound to the temples and idols of angry divinities. Freed from religion, they became agents of a radical new way of being that lived beyond the old distinctions of class, ethnicity and gender. In parallel with the liberal and inclusive pirate societies that grew up centuries later, early Christians believed that 'there is neither Jew nor Greek, slave nor free, male nor female…'[8] They took a similarly pirate view of property in that, in contrast to the enclosed personal fortunes of the few, they preached that in their community 'they held everything in common…'[9]

The religious authorities had preached (and still do) that life without an over-bearing God would lead to unbridled hedonism and the destruction of community. This is the same fear-filled message that was used to brand pirates as 'villains of all nations' – for if they lived outside of the authority of the church and state, then there would be no end to their depravity. In a similar way, early Christians were described in grotesque terms, and St Paul understood these accusations in his letters when he wrote that the Apostles had become 'the scum of the earth, the garbage of the whole world.'[10]

The message of the powerful has always been that without a 'big other' things would fall apart – best summarised in Dostoevsky's maxim that 'if God doesn't exist, everything is permitted.'[11] What pirates and these early Christian communities showed was that not only was this false, but that the opposite was true: it was in the name of omnipotent figures – Gods and monarchs – that endless violence and injustice had been done. Going to Golgotha, raising the Jolly Roger, living as if these deities were dead, released humanity to live as responsible for themselves and each other, rather than abdicated blame and responsibility for their actions onto a higher being.

We return again to Salvatore Maddi's conclusion:

> *'There are definite signs indicating when the psychotherapeutic process is complete...The capstone is when the client assumes responsibility for their own lives, despite all the outside pressures that can easily be blamed for what happens to them...'*[12]

This assumption of responsibility, this self-determination, lies right at the heart of the pirate spirit. The Atlantic pirates would no longer tolerate being alienated from the fruits of their labour, and those who rose up in the Midland Revolt wanted to resist the removal of responsibility for the land to some private owner. Maddi is talking here about the process of stepping out from under the enclosure of parental or familial pressure, but we can also see now how equally relevant it is for the move away from a life blocked by the 'big other' of religion too. The early Christians, like the Atlantic pirates, rejected the religious viewpoint that bound people to obedience and supplication and set them in their place in the order of things. By living as though this violent and angry God were dead, they re-released the radical message of the universal worth of all human beings, and thus were able to take full responsibility for their own actions. Far from being the rebels and retrogrades, the villains of all nations and scum of the whole earth, in pirates and early Christianity we see models of psychologically mature communities, living without separation anxieties and thus, like

Odysseus at the end of his travels, finally able to feel at home in the world.

Aliens and Tenants

The most obvious outworking of these beliefs was an acceptance of all, regardless of gender, ethnicity or social status, and a release of property back into the commons. This was fully in keeping with the message that Jesus had preached. His reading in the synagogue from the prophet Isaiah was one of his first public proclamations, and it in turn referenced verses from the early law book of the Old Testament, Leviticus. It is here that the principle of the 'jubilee year' is outlined: after every 7 cycles of 7 years, the land that the Israelites inhabited should be 'reset.' As the land had originally been partitioned fairly according to the families of the various tribes, this meant a regular fair redistribution of property rights. As God decrees in Leviticus 25:23, 'the land must not be sold permanently, because the land is mine and you are but aliens and my tenants.' In other words, there should be no permanent private enclosure. The economic separations that had been created should be torn down.

The principle went further than this, however. Beyond this periodic return of land to its original owners, debts were also cancelled, slaves and bonded servants were set free, the land was left fallow for it to recover and no work was to be done. A life of leisure and liberty, and the return of the commons to the people – the jubilee is truly pirate in its vision. It is a principle that Jesus chose to support in the opening words of his ministry, and one that the early Christians gathered around as they celebrated the death of the religions that had bound them.

Tragically - or inevitably - this radical kernel of Christianity was soon lost. Embraced by the Roman Empire as its official religion, within a few hundred years Christianity had become just as oppressive and legalistic as the Judaism its founder had subverted; by the time we reached 18th century England, the Christian religion was similarly synonymous with rich, powerful elites and self-serving clergy. Yet a radical element always remained, and the English revolutionaries of Captain Pouch's day employed the same jubilee teaching that Jesus and the early Christians had practiced as a way of campaigning against land expropriation. The Newcastle radical Thomas Spence penned a hymn to the tune of 'God Save the King' which ran:

Hark! How the trumpet's sound
Proclaims the land around
The Jubilee!
The sceptre now is broke,
Which with continual stroke,
The nations smote!
Hell from beneath doth rise,
To meet thy lofty eyes,
From the most pompous size,
Now brought to nought!
Since then this Jubilee
Sets all at Liberty
Let us be glad.
Behold each man return
To his possession
No more like drones to mourn
By landlords sad![13]

His lyrics were sung in taverns and hawked in pamphlets, even etched on walls, and by 1802 the Prime Minister was informed that barely a wall in London existed that did not have 'Spence's Plan and Full Bellies' chalked on it. Men did not want to be idle; they simply didn't want to be factory drones who were alienated from the rewards of their work. Their response to the capitalist mode of organising factory labour was to resurrect the ancient idea of the jubilee. It was similarly to this radical view of economics and social restructuring that the early Christian abolitionists turned when trying to rid the then developing world of the scourge of slavery - the separation of a person from their labour taken to the worst extreme. Robert Wedderburn, born in Jamaica in 1762 of a slave mother and slave-master father, mined the jubilee passages in particular when rousing up Jamaicans to revolt. Addressing Jamaican slaves, he knew that land ownership was central:

> *'Without [the land] freedom is not worth possessing; for if you once give up the possession of your lands, your oppressors will have power to starve you to death, through making laws for their own accommodation; which will force you to commit crimes in order to obtain subsistence.'*[14]

He also knew that this had been the experience of the poor thrown from enclosed land in England, which was likened to a man stealing another's handkerchief, and then employing him to embroider the new owner's initials on it. It was a quip nicely made, but one that rather trivialised the horrific reality of people being hung for protesting land enclosures and the high price of bread.

Though the jubilee principles were set out plainly to the Israelites, it appears that they were not followed properly, if at all. What is clear is that the land-owning father of the prodigal son story has a wealthy estate - which likely meant enclosed lands and hired, unlanded labourers to work it. He intends on handing this on to his sons, as he probably was handed it by his own father. The conservative message of the parable spoke of continuity in land ownership, not periodic redistribution - and the interpretation I have offered concerning this highlights this lack of sharing as a tragedy.

I can find no evidence that the Christians of the 18th Century understood this dark reading of the parable, but they certainly understood that the annual ritual of the stamping down of the boundaries was tied in heavily to this principle of jubilee, this symbolic return of the land to God - reaffirming it not as the landlord's private property, but as a common place in the public domain from which all could benefit.

It is a shame that they didn't, for taking this reading along with the psychological insights we now have into *The Odyssey*, we can see that the jubilee is also a regular act of remembrance not that the land belongs to some God from whom we are separated - for this separation is in fact a myth. Instead, it belongs to us all, in common, and when this commons comes under threat pirates - young heretics caring nothing for death or property or separations between sacred and profane - rise up to do their work of unblocking.

Or, at least, some do. For, as the story of the prodigal son teaches us, not all who sail out as pirates contribute to the strengthening of the commons. Some who begin as pirates but fail to follow through on their actions actually end up strengthening the empires of enclosure, and taking them on to another generation of oppression. Their selfish desires for wealth end up overriding the longing for justice that took them 'on the account.'

This is the classic story of the young music star, sampling and borrowing at will, raging against the structures that hold him back...who then slams eternal copyrights all over his work, and pursues other samplists with packs of lawyers.

It is the classic story of the freedom fighter turned tyrant – one that has played out in Cuba and China... and, one fears, will play out again in parts of the Arab world following the uprisings ignited by Mohamed Bouazizi.

And it is also the story of religions, so often begun by young idealistic pirates like Jesus or Mohammed – rebels convicted as heretics by the establishment – who break down the old religious enclosures around them and lead a group of disciples into a new place of freedom... who then, usually after the death of the founder, then go on to build more walls and enclosures, and commit more acts of barbarism as they protect their 'special' status. And so the Christian church moves from Peter saying to a beggar in the courts of the temple 'silver and gold have I none...' to the Pope – Peter's direct descendent, according to Catholics, who lives in the gilded opulence of the Vatican, sending out papal bull to control the lives of the faithful. If the prodigal son is the failed pirate individual, then religion is the failed pirate state: it is Libertatia turned Alcatraz.

This needs to be our note of caution then, for no matter how much we love pirates, and laud them for their brave acts beating the bounds, they remain ambiguous figures, violent, sometimes selfish, sometimes deeply flawed, often moving beyond the initial embrace of death to seek eternal significance. Beneath their fine clothes they, like all of us, wear the human dress. Not all of them will follow the fight through to liberty. Not all of them will lead us home again.

[*Pirate Baby Booties, £9.95*]

7

Captain You

'Going on the Account'

We have navigated numerous oceans in these preceding chapters, chasing pirates across vast expanses, then exploring tiny coves and rivulets, some of which may have felt far from home and, perhaps, caused some discomfort. We have sailed under a number of captains, all of whom have shown us what it is to live the pirate life, but one can only voyage so far as a passenger with pirates before the obvious question comes. Now the great crew of mutineers that we have followed falls silent, and turns to us. Some look desperately from gallows, others from darkened studios surrounded by amplifiers and cables. Still others stare out from rum-laden tables, or peer out from books, yet they all demand an answer to the same question: will *we* join them 'on the account?'

Having faced it themselves at some point they know, each of them, that the question was never an easy one to answer. For all time the pirate life has been hard - merry, yes, but lived at the margins, and likely to be cut short. And nor do they think that the answer is ever simple, for each pirate comes from his or her own world of troubles and battles, and each must choose for themselves. We are not poor brutalised sailors of 300 years ago, nor young black teenagers with no radio station to play and value *our* music. We are whoever we are, so as the pirates that surround us ask if we will go on the account with them, each of us must first ask this: what would it mean now to play pirate with the life that *I* have in the culture *I am* a part of, among the community *I* live in and within the power structures and working practices that *I am* embedded in?

Yet before we can answer that, a further question comes begging: are pirates even *needed* in these days? Are there still blockages and enclosures that need freeing up, people that need liberating, separations that need resisting and revolutions in self-determination that need igniting?

The *raison d'être* of this book is that we cannot simply answer that in the affirmative, but that we must do so urgently, for we are living in a world where the process of enclosure of the commons into private ownership is almost complete, and where separation from the essence of ourselves is marching ever onward. Like a cargo door that is rapidly closing, our hero running towards and beginning to roll under, the last chinks of light are still visible, but reducing with each passing day.

This is happening right across the spectrum of human experience, from our work to our creative arts to our social experiences to our religious expressions.

Playing Pirate At Work

We see it in the young people who feel increasingly trapped in the lives that are so quickly laden with debts that they are told they must shoulder if they are to become acceptable members of the educated, employable population. Nowhere has this been set out more clearly or more devastatingly than in Mark Fisher's book *Capitalist Realism*. Fisher, once a lecturer at a Further Education college in the UK, and now Visiting Fellow in the Centre for Cultural Studies at Goldsmiths University in London, writes from firsthand experience of the 'depressive hedonia' he witnessed among the student population. Depression is usually characterised by an inability to get pleasure; depressive hedonia, he writes, 'is an inability to do anything *except* get pleasure. There is a sense that 'something is missing' - but no appreciation that this mysterious, missing enjoyment can only be accessed beyond the pleasure principle.'[1] This student depression, he argues, stems from their realisation that they are like trapped animals. They know things are bad, but cannot do anything about it. They may as well live a merry life, as, while it may not be short, it is going to be one that is characterised by high levels of debt that must be incurred in order to get jobs which are no longer stable, to pay for houses which only their parents generation could afford, for whom they must pay more into their pensions and work until they are over 70 just to make ends meet. It is not that they are radicalised anti-capitalist protesters, simply that they see very clearly the end result of this long process of separation of labour and just reward. They are going to have to work, but they will see so little benefit from it.

Debt leaves a person enclosed by the system to whom it owes money. I left university with 'debts' of £300, which were easily cleared with a little temporary work over a summer vacation. I owed nobody, and was thus free to explore what I might want to do with my life. Leaving university now, young people can be faced with debt burdens of tens of thousands of pounds, the pressures of which simultaneously restricts the numbers who can afford to do non-vocational, yet highly important, subjects like philosophy, English or ancient history, and forces leavers to take whatever job they can lay their hands on, regardless of what their passions might be. How has it come to a situation, Fisher asks, where this has become an acceptable price for the continuation of a system that benefits so few and is hurting so many?

Atlantic piracy burst onto the seas as globalised capitalism was in its infancy. Pirates fought to wrestle control of ships from capitalists in order to overcome the separation they felt from their labour. Mutiny was not just about stepping out from under a brutal and violent regime, it was about reconnecting their work with the rewards that it brought. Now, as we struggle from one debt crisis to the next, with ultra-austere financial rescue packages foisted onto countries whose greatest mistake was to believe too readily the sales patter of the western banks who promised them so much, it is perhaps high time for pirates to emerge to challenge the basic and simple premises of the system of capital again. The pirates of the 18th century decided that they had had enough of being exploited, of their fate being torn from their hands. Remember: they did not turn to thievery as a way of getting wealthy, but simply changed the relationship between their labour and their economic return. As we have read: 'rather than work for meagre wages using the tools and machine (the ship) owned by a capitalist merchant, pirates commanded the ship as their own property and shared equally in the risk of their common adventure.[2]'

What this means is that going 'on the account' does not necessarily mean a rejection of work, or a rejection of positive economic activity, and nor does it mean advocating a communist alternative. Playing pirate to our capitalist economy does not require us to give up our jobs and live in hippy-style self-sufficient farming communes (though some might want to). What it does mean is thinking about changing the way we consider our labour, and changing our mindset from the dominant one that is concerned almost exclusively with personal profit. It means overcoming that economic separation, and trying to return to a system where work is *craft*, where our labour means something and is rewarded as such, even if those rewards are more modest than we might have grabbed in big business. To the bankers and merchants, those who do so will appear like zombies to them: economically dead, yet somehow still... too alive for comfort.

While it is vital that campaigns are sustained that lobby for changes to the ways financial institutions and markets are regulated, much of the focus of change needs to be at a more local level. Some might choose to set up their work as a collective, or simply engage their company in a serious conversation about employee-ownership schemes. Others might want to campaign for genuine improvements in income equality, while others might be in a position to consider changing details of copyright, or the relationship the company has with the public domain. Those involved in the arts need to think carefully about the connection that their work - their craft - has with 'the commons,' and how the body of work available to other artists to work with for free can be properly sustained.

For my own part, in the way I have published this book I have tried to take seriously the issues surrounding copyright and digital rights management. Part of the pirate spirit is about regaining control over the means of production so the hardback edition of this book has a cover which has been hand-printed – a nod to creating a unique product, and also as a way of exploring what the future of printed books might be in a digital age.

What people are increasingly coming to realise is that labour exploitation is not simply about trainers made in sweat-shops in the Far East. It is also about a culture that sees overwork as not only normal, but commendable. A culture that rewards backstabbing in business, and sends to positions of leadership those who commonly exhibit signs of psychopathy.[3] Hard work that is under a worker's control can be satisfying, and enjoyable. But hard work, with just a couple of weeks holiday each year, where overtime is expected, childcare is contracted out from too-busy parents to nurseries and minders and little control is given to the worker, is damaging. It is just that it is so endemic, so normalised, that we simply cannot see it any more.

Playing Pirate With Our Leisure

We need to consider how we can play pirate with our labour, but, more importantly, we need to consider how we can play pirate with our time in general. We have seen how the commons is the theatre upon which the rural community traditionally played out its life. While we have no realistic chance of changing land ownership by any significant degree - though there have been excellent campaigns that have won victories on the 'right to roam' in England - we should be proactive in promoting activities in which neighbourhoods can come together. The neighbourhood has always been the thorn in the flesh of the empire. It is at this local level that people are involved in gift relationships that are not exclusively about maximising profits. The old ritual of 'beating the bounds' is something that seems ripe for reinvention: an annual walk that teaches each new generation about the ownership rights of the land on which the community resides.

With the increasing technologisation of society we have been told that computers, and networked computers in particular, will make our lives easier, more relaxed and, with the labour savings they provide us, give us more time for leisure. If only this were true. Though the *correlation* between increased penetration of social networks and perceived increase in stress and busy-ness may not offer any definitive *causation,* what is quite clear is that we seem to be more tired and anxious about having so little time than ever before, and yet have found the time in our ever-more-busy schedules to spend more and more time grazing online, or scrolling through information about our friends on Facebook.

There is more to this than simply the amount of time that we are spending online - screen-time which is subtracted from the face-to-face time we might spend being fully present with children or significant others. The two major players in our online activity are Google and Facebook, both of which are totally free at the point of use. Yet both have enormous valuations on the stock market. What makes these sites so valuable is their ability to attract, then hold our attention, in the hope that we might be interested in the paid-for advertisements that appear in our peripheral vision. These ads are not randomly generated, but carefully selected using complex algorithms that draw on our past internet searches, the things our friends have 'liked', the status updates we have posted and the goods we have bought online. In order to hold our attention, and thus to hold their value, Google and Facebook require us to feed them information about ourselves. The sociologist Geert Lovink:

> *'We are honoured to be invited by the Machine to submit our opinions and preferences. We give in to the pressure to categorize data and join the swarms of 'collective intelligence.' Donate your*

wisdom to the crowds. We are invited to create reading lists, rank music and evaluate the products we consumed. User bees working for queen Google. It is so tempting to become part of the online 'pollination' world, as French economist Yann Moulier coined it, with billions of users acting like bees that fly from one website to the other, adding value for the owners.'[4]

These sites want us to spend more time browsing - and sell that time to us as good time, because it is time spent sharing with our friends or finding out new things - but, while their founders might talk a good game, the business people behind them know that it is time spent generating revenue and harvesting information that will lead to more focused advertising, which will generate more revenue even more efficiently. The writer Steven Johnson, who is about as technology-positive as it is possible to get, is equally worried by the enormous control that Facebook now has. In a recent article for *Wired* magazine, he wrote that 'with Facebook we are ultimately just tenant farmers on the land; we make it more productive with our labor, but the ground belongs to someone else.'[5]

The web, like the oceans, used to be seen as the great commons upon which we could all sail freely, and all enjoy liberation and benefit. What Johnson sees in Facebook is the virtual enclosure of that commons. While technically there is no reason why you cannot be on the internet without Facebook, when every single other person around is using the site the temptation to join in, rather than miss a party, is enormous.

The irony is that the best parties definitely happen offline. The Atlantic pirates, liberated from the strict controls on their time and labour, created 'TAZ' spaces - Temporary Autonomous Zones - in which they relaxed in liberated coves and allowed life to come to them, basking in all its enjoyment. We need to re-embrace this TAZ mentality. For us, though, Lovink thinks, the emphasis will not be so much on the 'Z' as on the 'T':

'In the past, emphasis was placed on creating spaces (such as parties and squats), while the TAZ of the contemporary age will emphasize the first element, it's temporary nature, and celebrate Chronos, the art of the longue durée. *After slow food, slow communication...'*[6]

The issue of efficient use of time drives right to the heart of our obsession with the market. To waste time is the ultimate sin. To waste time *and* resources and place oneself beyond the reach of conventional modes of communication - as both pirates and the prodigal son did - puts one beyond the pale. The Atlantic pirates broke the chains of their slavery and sailed to far-off islands, disconnecting themselves from normal social relations in the process. So perhaps to play pirate now and pursue TAZ in the midst of the busy-ness of hard work and hard browsing would be to *not* surf the oceans of the net, to not let the net 'serf' us, and reject constant status-updates, 'check-ins' and always-on communication with others.

Playing Pirate With the Media

Pirates, however, were not Luddites. They didn't reject technological progress as inherently bad. Rather, they resisted the use of technology to oppress them and further alienate them from the wealth that their labour created. So, while playing pirate with the capitalist mindset of our world might mean some disengagement from sites that seek to harvest our content in order to sell us more products, what it will also mean is more intelligent appropriation and control of that technology. Projects like *Diaspora*[7] are trying to do exactly that with the creation of an open-source, privacy-aware set of social networking tools which allow users to create, manage and own their own 'hubs', without the need for advertisements or other revenue-generation factors. Levink again:

> *'There are political reasons to support such initiatives. I don't want to overstate the CIA's role, but it is well known that activists must be very cautious using Facebook. For a while it was OK to spread the message for this or that campaign, but Facebook is becoming too dangerous as an internal channel to coordinate civil disobedience. [...] Let's strengthen the self-determination of the nodes against the cloud's central authority and keep the Web decentralized.'*[8]

Resistance to centralised authority is pure pirate behaviour, and 'self-determination of nodes' is simply digital speak for 'crew-managed ships.' Although Google and Facebook both have very laudable founders who seem genuinely to want to 'do no evil' and 'make the world a more connected place' (as their corporate mottos go) they do now wear the same mantle that the Guild of Printers once did. They are permitted to go about their business, and make themselves fabulously wealthy, but in return for the government's permission to do this, they must do some snooping, and censor any elements that are seen as subversive. Let us also be clear: their aggressive strategy of buying up smaller, more inventive rivals is analogous to the smashing of Henry Hill's non-guild printing presses. Those who offer truly free alternatives can expect those with money to try to smash them.

What might surprise someone adopting a system such as Diaspora would be the sort of information they found out about those they were connected to. What Facebook does is use a sophisticated series of algorithms to decide which of our friends' updates we see first. When we log on, the list we see is not strictly chronological, but ranked according to other factors too. (At the time of writing, Facebook was experimenting with being able to 'pay to promote posts' - which would mean friends would see your update bumped up to the top of their list.)[9] We are not consciously aware of how these algorithms work, or what information they might be hiding from us. When we buy a newspaper, we are likely to be more aware of the fact that it is edited, and that the information we are seeing has been chosen according to some editorial policy. Indeed, we tend to buy our papers based on this policy, because we feel it matches our own.

What the recent investigations into the tabloid media in the UK have shown is that the information we got through these papers was often utterly fabricated, or, perhaps worse, obtained through illegal means, with people's mobile phones and other personal data being hacked into. Whilst we have always expected a level of editorial bias in the media we consume, the News International scandal, and the Leveson inquiry that it precipitated, have highlighted the limited extent to which our 'free' press is really 'free,' and our politicians are really acting solely for the good of the country.

Playing pirate with the media will also mean reassessing our relationship to the media that we consume and/or produce. For those in the music business piracy can, quite understandably, feel like a terrible threat. But, challenging though it is, the apparently new world of payment for performance and limited income from recording sales is actually a return to what has always been more 'normal.' It was only in the few decades from the 1950's when recording, distribution and playback technologies came together to allow artists like The Rolling Stones and Led Zeppelin to earn huge sums from music because it was effectively 'enclosed' by vinyl. That was an aberration. Things will never be the same again, and that may turn out to be a very good thing for creativity in the longer term, although we are clearly a long way from clear water on the issue.

For all of us who consume music and film, we too need to consider what the best approach is going to be. Some may feel no compunction about downloading Rolling Stones tracks for free, but want to pay for music by newer artists, and even pay a great deal for artisan vinyl releases. Others may want to challenge the Digital Rights Management code that blights many works and prevents their free use by those who've paid good money for them. Others still may want to explore outfits like Records on Ribs who are modelling new ways of distributing music and charging for it.

As with all of our media consumption, we need to be more reflective, and not dumb consumers - challenging where we feel corporations *or* file-sharers are not serving the public best. The 'pirate publishers' like Henry Hill subverted the official disseminators of information by providing a critique of the ruling classes, and opinion on important issues of the day at a price that 'commoners' could afford. We now have incredible technologies at our disposal that mean we can share information to a wide audience for very little cost. People are already playing pirate with the mainstream media, and they have had to respond in kind. But we must make sure that in a world of information overload, we give proper time to real news stories about the lives of real people facing real injustices - and not just to endless updates about what our friends did last night.

Playing Pirate With Our Desires

One of the dangers of information overload is that we spend so long trying to stop ourselves drowning in news about other people that we end up knowing nothing about ourselves. Any time for self-reflection tends to be the first thing that goes when pressure mounts, because it is largely perceived as time wasted. The social networks that have come to dominate the way so many relationships are facilitated have brought enormous benefits, but the window that they bring onto other people's lives also functions as a looking glass into our own. As such, we can feel anxious about how we are being seen, and end up spending inordinate amounts of time tending our social network pages with the right sorts of photos and comments and lists of interests so that other people might find us acceptable and desirable.

Whether it is parents or other significant people who might cause us to feel anxious about our own worth, we need, like Wendy, to understand the things that may be blocking our way to emotional maturity. The ideas of French psychoanalyst Jacques Lacan speak directly into this situation. Lacan's first, and most important, publication was 'The Mirror Stage' in 1936. In this he outlines what is happening when, somewhere between the ages of six and eighteen months, a baby will recognise themselves in a mirror. Prior to this stage, they will likely be able to recognise their parents or siblings in a mirror image and understand that this image of the other person is not *actually* them, but the moment that they recognise *themselves* in the mirror is, according to Lacan, hugely significant. The writer Lionel Bailly explains:

> *'When it recognises itself in the mirror, the child already knows that this image is not the 'real person'; unlike a monkey, who may try to attack the image as a rival, the baby understands almost immediately its unreality, while experiencing powerfully through this unreality that wholeness of itself for the first time - 'this is not me, and yet this is me.'*[10]

Thus, from this time, the baby has an evolving understanding that their identity is both 'what I am' and 'what others and I see of me'. As Bailly continues, 'the image is oneself and simultaneously not oneself, and no sooner has there been this splitting, than there is a merging and confusion of subject and object.'

In a world so dominated by the visual, this fragmenting and confusing tension between the self that I feel within me and the self that I feel others seeing of me, can cause deep-seated anxiety. With social networks, and the explosion of photo-sharing on all sorts of websites, we are now forced to reflect on how we see ourselves as others see us hundreds of times more each day than Lacan or any of his contemporaries. With each new image there can be another tiny separation, another splitting, another distancing of the 'I' that I might feel is within me and the 'me' that others experience. For Lacan, this means that the desires that we grow up with are not actually our own desires, but the inherited desires of our parents and significant others around us. (This is perhaps best seen in fashion, where we desire certain things, essentially because people we respect around us desire them.) As Lacan understood and practised it, 'what psychoanalysis reveals is that human-beings need to learn how, and what, to desire.'[11]

Part of this process of understanding what our true desires should be will have an impact on our awareness of ourselves as consumers. So much of our consumption – the new cars we insist we deserve, or the new shoes we think will finally make us happy – is about an attempt to overcome the sense of fracture and insecurity that we feel when we consider how others view us, as well as about the desires that we have inherited from our parents.

We have already examined how we might begin to challenge some of the unhelpful systemic aspects of capitalism, but the greater work is always going to be about beginning to control our desires to consume more. We are capitalists first and foremost not because of the economic systems we are a part of, but because of the desires we have to profit, to win, and to gather more resources to ourselves. It is to this work of becoming more satisfied not just with *who we are*, but with *what we have*, that we must commit ourselves.

This work towards inner contentment may involve simple reflection on economic inputs and outputs, and what is fair and just. It might also involve practices such as meditation, which is one way of exploring at a deep level this Lacanian process of revealing how, and what, to desire. Or, as Bailly puts it:

> *'Psychoanalysis is about accompanying the patient towards his/her subjective truth, or towards the point where the objective 'me' and the subjective 'I' can be united.'*[12]

As anyone who has been through psychotherapy will testify, this can be a painful, yet hugely rewarding process. Examining and rejecting the desires that we may have taken from our parents and peers can seem frightening, confusing, or somehow 'wrong.' This is the storm in which Wendy finds herself as *Peter Pan* opens: unable to discern clearly between who she wants to be, and who her father wants her to become. It is the pirates in the story that give her permission to step out of the blocked world of Neverland, where she is becoming nothing at all, and to actually go into battle with her desires - which leads her to symbolically slaying her father in the figure of Captain Hook. Through this heretical act of patricide she is finally able to break free and go some way to uniting her subject and object. Pirates, once again, are at work to overcome the separations that lead people away from an integrated sense, not just of their labour, but of themselves too.

For some of us, we need to take courage from the pirates that we find lurking in films, books and plays, and let them lead us into battles with the desires that present themselves to us in the fragments of mirror images we see in our screens every day. The road to emotional maturity is a tough one, but in a world where depression, anxiety and mental illness are on the rise, it is one that needs treading and opening up. This need not mean work with a professional therapist - though any stigma that still surrounds seeing a therapist needs to be quashed - but it will mean a better understanding of self-reflection and the wide dissemination of tools for talking peaceably through where things may have gone wrong in the past within family relationships.

For others of us, we will need a different sort of courage. For those of us who are parents, we will need to be brave enough to allow our children to commit heresy against us. We have, in all likelihood, prepared the ground for this in our willingness for our children to dress up as pirates or other 'deviant' characters. What we must then be prepared to accept is that we will have made mistakes, and that, in order to come to a more full and mature relationship with us, we may need to be symbolically slain with cutlasses, or peppered with grape shot so that our children can step out from our shadows and find their own true desires.[13]

Playing Pirate With Our Beliefs

This will be painful work, I'm sure. But it is vital that we allow ourselves to be vanquished as a way of killing off the desire that might remain in us to overcome our own disappointments by subsuming the lives of our children and living through them. The story of the prodigal son is terribly important, for we all need to resist the temptation to conserve our own empires through the sacrificial offering of our children's passions.

Perhaps the most famous 'tragic prodigal' story is that of Michael Corleone. In Mario Puzo's classic novel *The Godfather* we see him, this young Corleone son, trying to resist involvement in his father's empire, only to find himself increasingly enmeshed in cycles of bloody violence and sacrificial retribution. Following his revenge killing of a drug king-pin and a corrupt policeman, Michael flees to Sicily, where he falls in love with the beautiful Apollonia. It seems that a woman will, as in *The Odyssey*, bring some peaceful resolution to the story and save Michael from becoming snared in his father's business, but she is killed in a car bomb intended for

Michael and he returns to New York, hell bent on wiping out rival families and extending the brutal regime he had once so hated.

The violence of *The Godfather* presents as particularly shocking as it is not waged as part of a struggle for freedom, but in order to punish and keep a grip on power. Much as Michael may want to play pirate with his family, and go in search of a new life, it quickly becomes apparent that his attempt is destined to fail as his father's desires within him for bloody revenge are greater than his own desire for peace. Defence of the family honour, and feeling comfortable with the robes and rings, highlights that the blood of the Ma fia – 'my thing' – runs deep.

The old game of the Mafia is the racket of protection: by keeping up regular payments, businesses can be kept safe - because who knows what evil forces might bear down if the Mafia weren't around? The truth is, of course, that it will be the protectors *themselves* who will mete out punishment. The payments are a way of sustaining protection from the protectors. If the protectors were suddenly not around, there would simultaneously be nothing to be protected from.

In tragic figures like Michael we see the pirate archetype not being followed through to completion, and thus we see characters who cannot properly individuate. Because they can't properly individuate, they can't overcome the tension between the desires that their families feed into them, and their own desires. They never learn how, or what, to desire.

So here, in *The Godfather*, in the Mafia model of business, we see Puzo's re-telling of the prodigal tragedy reflecting back on the tragedy of Western Christianity, a religion that has turned Jesus into the God-Father - a supposedly goodly figure who demands sacrifice and veneration in return for protection from the terrible forces of evil, while preaching that it is that same father who will cast into hell those who refuse to pay up.

In his book *Redeeming Nietzsche* the theologian Giles Fraser (who was recently caught up in the Occupy protests encamped around St Paul's Cathedral) wrote that 'Christianity has spread a disease of self-hate simply in order to sell itself as the cure.'[14] I must be very *very* bad, in other words, if only a God *that* powerful can save me. This is the extraordinary construct of evangelicalism, and all religious extremism: the more a religion is able to demonstrate just how bad people are, the more it can promote their God as the one who is so powerful 'he' can save.

This view tends to become nuanced among those towards the centre of the churches or fundamentalist communities: it is not necessarily that *I* am so bad, because I am actually a very good person who does all sorts of good works and lives a good life. Rather, it is that there are people out there who I can point to who are very very bad that prove that God must be very very powerful. Thus the 'depravity' of homosexuals or those who have abortions, or Muslims, or Jews, or blacks, or women with loose morals, is oddly fetishised, because it helps create a vision of God who is even more powerful. This is why 'witness' services are so important in these communities, because it is in the telling of these awful tales that people are again convinced of God's great goodness in drawing people out of such great badness.

Pirates were denigrated as 'villains of all nations' - strung up as examples of the worst scum the earth contained. Separated from families, living as hedonistic communities of men, not attending church - pirates were the very very bad that an anxious and puritan church needed in order to project the image of a terribly powerful God to keep the faithful in line. And yet the truth about them was far removed from this monstrous picture, for these pirates were simply those who refused to play the same protection racket game that the Mafia still use now. Told that their apostasy would lead to their death and damnation, they raised their Jolly Rogers and lived as ones *already* dead and damned. They stepped out from under the fire and brimstone, from under the curses and threats of their barbaric employers, from under the rule of merchants and princes, and decided that they were free men and women.

In a world where fundamentalism - religious and atheist - is increasing, we once again need people who are brave enough to play pirate to belief. It will not be an easy path to take, for we know that playing pirate with powerful systems of belief or governance raises them to violence. Those who still have so much to gain perpetuating the separation myth, the bogey-man behind the curtain, will once again look to hunt down those who preach radical freedom, and string them up on raw wooden beams in the shadows of their grand temples.

Two pirates strung up ready to be hung in 1718 made the cry that 'a pirate's life is the only life of a man of any spirit.' And this should be the cry of the modern 'pirates of the charism' too. For Slavoj Žižek, the Holy Spirit who comes after Jesus' death is no more than the animus of a community living out the theological reality that the separation that they had thought existed no longer does. The 'many tongues' of Pentecost, and the heretical apostles who suffered for speaking them, are again the 'villains of all nations,' and it will take people of all creeds, and none, to speak carefully this truth that our fragmented and desire-ridden selves find so difficult to accept: that the violent and angry God, who frightens us into line with threats of punishment and who is only pacified by bloody sacrifice, is dead. This sacred spirit within humanity that Žižek would say is born from this death is perhaps then the pirate within us all, the Jolly Roger bumper sticker that is the scent of an ancient and vital knowledge that enclosure is not the way that life should be lived. This holy spirit is the skull and crossed-bones baby grow that is the mark of becoming death to the systems of oppression, in order to become agents of change that can resurrect new life. And this divine spirit is the plastic eye patch that is the mark of those who know that deeply and thus, with their sight restored, can begin to live as integrated people once again.

Conclusion: Overcoming Separation

Sailing in the wake of Telemachus, of Blackbeard, of Henry Hill and Captain Pouch and Anne Bonny, it is us who now face the telling question: who will go on the account and play pirate to the blocked systems we find ourselves enmeshed in? Who will take cutlasses to the our politics, our music, our economics, our ecology and get under our skins and into the hearts of our selves and right down to our souls?

With their flag on our clothes, their costumes in our children's parties, their descendants still fighting in Somalia and hacking the internet, we might rightly ask, what is it with pirates? And now, after all these oceans, we have our answer: pirates emerge in merry battle to do battle against enclosure and separation. Hundreds of years after the Atlantic pirates were slaughtered, Karl Marx wrote his great treatise on capitalism, and the problem of our alienation from our labour. The pirates who took control of their own ships were the first over the top in the battle against the enclosing and divisive scourge unfair labour. Yet what Marx failed to understand was that capitalism was not simply an *external* set of systems, but an *internal* set of values which spoke sweetly to the human heart that has, from early life, seen an image of itself in the mirror and struggled to find wholeness.

Religions have sought to speak to these internal separations and work to draw us away from our tendency towards narcissism and selfishness. However, they have so often been in bed with the power structures they felt they depended on, churches too often failed to challenge the external systems of separation that Marx had identified, and were oppressed as heretical if they did. We might then argue that in their separate failings, capitalism and Christianity have been the two great forces that have worked to separate us from core parts of what it is to be human.

Yet these twin failures are taken up and re-integrated in the work of pirates, who spring from coves and out of books, from spaceships and radio stations to fight against economic separation and personal alienation, and do battle externally and internally for the integration of the human spirit.

In his book *First as Tragedy, then as Farce*, Žižek writes:

> *'The enclosure of the commons is a process of proletarianization of those who are excluded from their own substance... The present conjecture compels us to radicalise it to an existential level well beyond Marx's imagination. We need a more radical notion of the proletarian subject.'*[15]

If we have been excluded from our own substance, then it is the enclosures of capitalism and institutional Christianity that have created these separations. This true substance of humanity *is* 'the commons,' which, in the end, is the physical, ethical, spiritual and sociological gravity that draws us away from individualism and selfishness, from the endless pursuit of profits and the tireless denigration of the marginalised into community and mutual dependency.

In all areas of life - physical, intellectual, spiritual, ecological and social - these commons are under threat, and so in all of these areas of life we need pirates to run up their Jolly Roger, rise up once more and defend them.

Who will play pirate to the blocked religions that keep so many miserable? Who will have the courage to face the inevitable violence, the familiar exclusion and belittlement, the likely economic cost and the fury of the powerful? Who will stand up to defend the commons from the march of private enclosure, our radical beliefs from the prison of fundamentalism, where the shared right of action has been diminished to the domain of a professional, clerical elite?

The Jolly Roger and the three masts of Golgotha... The skull and crossbones and the place of the skull... Christianity in its most radical and true form is the pirate religion that embraces the death of all religion. It was founded by a man who stands fully in the pirate tradition. Born into a poor family, he experienced first hand the oppressive violence and brutality of a political and religious regime that was designed to draw wealth to the centre and keep the powerful in power. The Pharisees and Sadducees kept an uneasy pact with their Roman occupiers: they could practice their religion freely, as long as they paid their taxes and did not criticise Roman rule. Jesus went 'on the account' and refused to comply by these rules. He lived life as a 'TAZ', knowing that violent retribution would pursue him, for those who lived freely and exposed the power of empire and religion as empty could not be allowed to live. After a piratic raid on the Temple courts, one of his number was tempted by silver and he was betrayed. His bones broken, raised on a cross at the place of the skull, he performed the 'dance to the four winds' alongside two other common criminals.

And yet, though his message has been sterilised and gutted into institutional nonsense, his dance continues to challenge others to fight against oppression. Who will strike the sails again, rip the curtains and tear down the veils that have kept churches such barren and infertile places? If cleanliness is next to godliness, then the death of this sterile god is a welcome invasion of revitalising dirt into the spiritual place.

All of these separations - economic and spiritual - have been extraordinarily damaging to our planet and to our people. Yet this is why pirates remain such powerful figures in our cultural imagination, for it is pirates who finally live out, in their short but merry lives, the fact that the human spirit will *not* stand to be bought, sold or defeated.

It has been my contention here that if we in the developed world are to restore something of our dignity, then we do need a revival of piratic action to draw us away from further economic alienation. The 99% need to feel again that their work is craft, that their labour has a wider meaning than propping up the stock price to make bankers rich. This will require a new spirit to challenge the encroachment of market economics into the lives of communities, and renewed ways of doing work that resist the singular pursuit of profit. Moreover, we need to create legislation that will return the idea of copyright to that of stimulating innovation while pumping life into the public domain.

But, far more importantly, we need to see that the work that pirates must do is as much internal as external. We might suffer separation and alienation from our labour, but beyond the battle to create a more just economics in the privatised and enclosed West, we need a more radical notion of ourselves. This is where Odysseus and Jesus, our pirates of the divine, our pirates of the inner self, are so vitally important. For with a merry cry and in rowdy shanty voice they go beyond Marx's materialism, rise up in beautiful religious mutiny and, in their dangerous liberty, expose the myth of our most basic separation:

we are already whole,

we are already home,

we are already good.

London – Sheffield – Lucca, June 2012

Postscript

When I began to write and think about pirates I had no idea that they would capture me quite so significantly and genuinely take me 'on the account.'

The book has been a slight departure from the other non-fiction works I have published. It is, on the surface, not as strictly theologically minded. Under the surface though, I believe that this is perhaps the most deeply theological work I have written. Not that that should be taken to mean that it is grounded in more orthodox belief... This has been a highly personal journey through some very tough territory, and I'm hugely grateful to the friends and family around me who have supported me, believed me and believed in me, even as belief has waned, as this book has become written. I may not write another like it; my heart, for now, is heading to fiction.

As those who follow my writing will know, in the writing of this book I decided that its publication needed to be in the same spirit as that of its subject, which is why I chose to turn down the 'normal' publishers and turn to self publishing. In doing so I have been able to place a 'stinted copyright' on the text, which will be released into the public domain after a certain time, when I've gained a little private compensation for the time and resources I've put into this.

Thanks to the one who sang me back into myself.

τῃ του εμου καρδια σ ληστῃ

For further information please visit *kesterbrewin.com*.

Notes

Chapter 1 – Captain Roberts

[1] Redicker, M., Villains Of All Nations, Beacon Press, 2004, p 10

Chapter 2 – Captain Teach

[1] Johnson, Captain C., *A General History of the Robberies & Murders of the Most Notorious Pirates*, Conway Maritime Press, 2002, p 57

[2] ibid., 81

[3] Thucydides 1, 5

[4] Redicker, M., *Villains Of All Nations*, Beacon Press, 2004, p 25

[5] ibid., 174

[6] ibid., 4

[7] ibid., 43

[8] ibid., 44

[9] Johnson, Captain C., *A General History of the Robberies & Murders of the Most Notorious Pirates*, Conway Maritime Press, 2002, p 180

[10] Redicker, M., *Villains Of All Nations*, Beacon Press, 2004, p 70

[11] Johnson, Captain C., *A General History of the Robberies & Murders of the Most Notorious Pirates*, Conway Maritime Press, 2002, p 60

[12] Bey, H., T.A.Z, Autonomedia, New York, 2003, p 109

[13] Lamborn Wilson, P., *Pirate Utopias: Moorish Corsairs and European Renegadoes*, Autonomedia, 2003, p 194 (Lamborn Wilson is an alter-ego of Hakim Bey)

[14] See Balázs, B., *A Short History of Book Piracy*, in Media Piracy in Emerging Economies, Social Science Research Council publication, p. 408

[15] ibid.

[16] Latterly, organised gangs have begun to muscle in in a far more violent way on the hijacking business, using bonded labour in much the same way as the old navies did - so the theory I am proposing here does not extrapolate to condone or theorise their activity in any way, other than this: where money can be made, even by the poor, the powerful will muscle in and take the reins for their own benefit.

[17] Langewiesche. W., *The Pirate Latitudes*, Vanity Fair, April 2009

Chapter 3 – Captain Pouch

[1] Hyde, L., *Common As Air*, Farrar, Straus and Giroux, 2010, p 31.

[2] ibid., 41

[3] ibid., 25

[4] We aren't told much in *Charlie and the Chocolate Factory* about the Oompa-Loompas' attitude to their enslaved labour, other than they gave up their freedom because of their love of chocolate and hatred of large insects, and were rather mischievous and subversive. In the Harry Potter series, we do know that Hermione Granger campaigned for better rights for elves - who worked for nothing in the Hogwarts' kitchens, or as pained, bonded slaves to wizards, and that Harry Potter freed one elf, Dobby - which resulted in great misery and social anxiety for the elf concerned. These are the almost-silent great host of worker-drones, who labour to provide sustenance to their anxieties about empire and power.

[5] Hyde, L., *Common As Air*, Farrar, Straus and Giroux, 2010, p 88

[6] Interestingly, this resistance to authority, this refusal to take the abuses thrown at them was the direct inspiration for the workers' rights movements which came later. The word 'strike' was originally used in relation to labour in 1768, when, in support of demonstrations in London, sailors 'struck' - removed - the topsails of ships at port, thus rendering them immobile. Although piracy had been virtually eliminated by then by the brutal regime of hangings, sailors still saw pirates as role models who had resisted the terrible conditions in which they still worked. The strike became a form of TAZ: a temporary rejection of labour, a small bubble of liberty in which our work is not owned by the capitalists, but remains our own to withdraw. Though no longer going the full way to turning pirate by declaring mutiny on board, to strike was to move symbolically in that direction, so that sailors reminded ship owners that they could still turn pirate if they so wanted.

[7] Redicker, M., *Villains Of All Nations*, Beacon Press, 2004, p 44

[8] ibid., 146

[9] ibid.

[10] ibid., 169

Chapter 4 – Captain Newport

[1] Linebaugh, P., *The Many-Headed Hydra: The Hidden History of the Revolutionary Atlantic*, Verso, 2000, p 8

[2] ibid., 30

[3] See http://www.bartleby.com/5/104.html

[4] Hyde, L., *Common As Air*, Farrar, Straus and Giroux, 2010, p 119

[5] ibid., 57

[6] It's therefore somewhat ironic that Jagger chose to take the name of his band from the Bob Dylan song, 'Like A Rolling Stone,' - which is about poverty and having no roof over one's head, or food to put on the table at all.

[7] For some lovely background to this, check out Keith Richards writing to his Aunt Patty about meeting Mick Jagger for the first time - and the connection they made over US blues artists that they loved: http://www.lettersofnote.com/2012/04/he-is-called-mick-jagger.html

[8] See: http://www.piratpartiet.se/international/english

[9] For an excellent analysis of this process, see the *This American Life* episode 'When Patents Attack': http://www.thisamericanlife.org/radio-archives/episode/441/when-patents-attack

[10] See: http://minnesota.publicradio.org/display/web/2009/02/06/pirates/

[11] See: http://gigaom.com/2012/01/31/neil-young-is-right-piracy-is-the-new-radio/

[12] http://www.guardian.co.uk/music/2012/mar/17/punk-rock-state-oppression-burma?CMP=twt_iph

[13] Jung, C., *Modern Man in Search of a Soul*, London, Routledge, p 205.

Chapter 5 – Captain Hook

[1] Jung, C., *Modern Man in Search of a Soul*, London, Routledge, p 207.

[2] ibid.

[3] A scene at the end of *The Empire Strikes Back*. Any neek will tell you the timecode if you need it ;-)

[4] Maddi, S., *The Quest for Human Meaning*, London, Routledge, 1998, p 9

[5] ibid., 23

Chapter 6 – Captain Odysseus

[1] *The Odyssey*, Book 9, 408-411; 461-463 (Penguin Edition, 1996, translated by Robert Fagles)

[2] Rollins, P., *The Idolatry of God*, (forthcoming)

[3] *The Odyssey*, Book 16, 215 – 217 (Penguin Edition, 1996, translated by Robert Fagles)

[4] Luke 15:32

[5] Luke 16:9

[6] Redicker, M., *Villains Of All Nations*, Beacon Press, 2004, p 125

[7] Žižek, S., and Milbank, J., The Monstrosity of Christ – Paradox or Dialectic?, Cambridge, MIT Press, 2009, p. 81

[8] Galatians 3:28

[9] Acts 2:44

[10] 1 Corinthians 4:13

[11] Dostoevsky, Fyodor, *The Brothers Karamazov*, (Part IV, Book XI, Ch 4.)

[12] Maddi, S., *The Quest for Human Meaning*, London, Routledge, 1998, p 23

[13] Linebaugh, P., *The Many-Headed Hydra: The Hidden History of the Revolutionary Atlantic*, Verso, 2000, p 292

[14] Redicker, M., *Villains Of All Nations*, Beacon Press, 2004, p 314

Chapter 7 – Captain You

[1] Fisher, M., *Capitalist Realism - Is There Any Alternative?*, Zero Books, London, 2009, p. 22

[2] Redicker, M., *Villains Of All Nations*, Beacon Press, 2004, p 70

[3] See, for example, http://www.guardian.co.uk/science/2011/sep/01/psychopath-workplace-jobs-study

[4] Lovink, G., *Networks Without A Cause - A Critique of Social Media*, Polity Press, Cambridge, 2011, p. 25

[5] See: http://www.wired.com/epicenter/2012/05/mf_facebook/

[6] Lovink, G., *Networks Without A Cause - A Critique of Social Media*, Polity Press, Cambridge, 2011, p. 29

[7] See: http://diaspora.github.com/diaspora/

[8] Lovink, G., *Networks Without A Cause - A Critique of Social Media*, Polity Press, Cambridge, 2011, p. 31

[9] See: http://www.bbc.co.uk/news/technology-18033259

[10] Bailly, L., *Lacan*, One World Press, Oxford, 2009, p. 30

[11] See the entry on Lacan at The Internet Encyclopaedia of Philosophy: http://www.iep.utm.edu/lacweb/#SH2b

[12] Bailly, L., *Lacan*, One World Press, Oxford, 2009, p. 35

[13] There may be economic aspects to this too. The 'baby boomer' generation born in the decade or so after World War 2 are now approaching retirement. Their children are now approaching their 30's or 40's, and yet they are finding things far harder than their parents did. House prices have exploded beyond the reach of many, and while their baby boomer parents are retiring on very generous packages, those who follow them know that they will have to work longer and pay more to receive pensions that are still nowhere near as good. Tough though it may be to take, baby boomer parents may have to take courage and downsize from their often vast, echoing houses that no longer run with voices of full families in order to help their children.

[14] Fraser, G., *Redeeming Nietzsche - On the Piety of Unbelief*, Routledge, London, 2002, p. 73

[15] Žižek, S., *First As Tragedy, Then As Farce,* Verso, London, 2009, p. 92